THE SCORPION'S SWEET VENOM

THE SCORPION'S SWEET VENOM

Diary of a Brazilian Call Girl

Bruna Surfistinha

Interviewed by Jorge Tarquini
Translated by Alison Entrekin

BLOOMSBURY

First published in Brazil by Panda Books, 2005

First published in Great Britain 2006

Copyright © 2005 by Raquel Pacheco

Translation copyright © 2006 by Alison Entrekin

The moral right of the author
and translator has been asserted

Bloomsbury Publishing Plc,
36 Soho Square, London W1D 3QY

A CIP catalogue record for this book
is available from the British Library

ISBN 0 7475 8801 5
ISBN-13 9780747588016

Typeset by Hewer Text UK Ltd, Edinburgh
Printed in Great Britain by Clays Ltd, St Ives plc

PROLOGUE

A beautiful day dawned. I don't know why, but something happens inside me when the sun shines on a cold day. Everything feels unreal, as if I'm in a waking dream: that bright light in the blue sky that doesn't heat up. A beautiful lie. This was the first thing I saw when I woke up at ten o'clock in the morning. Soon the enchantment of this dreamlike scenario gave way to the reality of my dilemma. Was this really what I wanted to do with my life? I knew that if I left it would be for ever. There would be no going back. Not for me or my parents.

I packed a few items of clothing into my school-bag. I couldn't walk out of there with a suitcase. As I was going through my wardrobe, I saw so many beautiful clothes and was sad I couldn't take all of them. I packed some underwear, pyjamas, a T-shirt, a top, a few bikinis to work in and, along with the clothes on my body and a coat, my luggage was ready. My little cat just watched. I tried to hide her in my bag, but she didn't like the idea. Well, I thought, another thing I have to leave behind, along with my designer clothes, bedroom and memories.

I went into the living room and sat at the dining table, pretending to do my homework. I was really watching my mother, silent, with her back to me, making something in the kitchen. I recognised that she didn't deserve to go through all that. But it was what I wanted to do. Or had to do. I sat there thinking that in a short space of time she had lost two daughters. My oldest sister (who was also my godmother) had never come back from America.

I was euphoric on the one hand, but sad on the other. Watching that woman, who once upon a time had given up her own life to get married and look after a house and kids, including me, who wasn't her natural daughter, I felt a strong urge to tell her about my decision. To show her that none of this was because of her, but me. I could even follow in her footsteps and sacrifice myself, do everything she had done . . . No. I'd made my decision.

I started writing everything I wanted to tell her on the piece of paper in front of me. It wasn't pre-meditated. It was spontaneous and sincere, in a way that I hadn't been for a long time. I thanked her for everything she'd done for me, asked her to forgive me for the pain she'd feel, but made it clear that I was going to seek my own happiness, wherever that might be. I hoped that this would mean she and my father could be happy again, without me, without my problems. I reread the letter, which looked like a suicide note. I was unable to write things differently, however. In a way, something was dying in me that day.

I left the letter on the table and got my file and schoolbag. I always left through the kitchen door. I passed my mother, leaning against the sink. 'Bye, Mum.' She didn't answer. She didn't turn round. I knew I'd never see her again. I stood in the doorway for a moment, looking at her. Still she didn't turn round. I really regret the hug I didn't have the courage to give her at that moment. I love my mum. She didn't know it. She didn't turn round. There was no word, no gesture. From either of us. In silence, I closed the door behind me. Bye, Mum.

The intercom rings. He's here! While he's coming up in the lift, I go over the last few details: hair brushed, perfumed skin, mouth ready for anything and everything. In the bedroom, the bed is ready, the light soft. To set the atmosphere, I put on a CD (if the guy's a bore, I play something mellow, or techno if I want to liven things up; if he's nice, I prefer Jota Quest, Emerson Nogueira, something more romantic). I'm wearing a really short, provocative skirt and a top that shows off my breasts. All easy to take off. Or have taken off. I'm wearing stilettos. Not that I mind being short. It's part of my charm. The doorbell rings. I let him in. He kisses me on the cheek and introduces himself, since this is his first time with me. Although I don't have to, I do the same. I take his hand and lead him to the sofa. We chat as if we were on a date but the conversation soon gets dirty.

'Today I want to give it to you from behind.'
'But do you want my cunt or my arsehole?'

'Everything,' he whispers in my ear, while his hand roams my thighs.

His mouth brushes against my neck and I can feel his unshaven face. My hands between his legs make him go rock hard. He tugs my top down and my tits pop out. He's like a kid with a new toy; I let him squeeze them firmly, but gently. My nipples go hard as his tongue glides around them. His breathing is hot and heavy. He licks one breast, then the other, then squeezes them together, trying to fit them both in his mouth like a greedy boy. In the jumble of quickly removed clothes, he pulls down my knickers and runs his tongue down to my belly button. Then he stops and gives me a cheeky look.

'Do you want me to go down on you?'

'Yes.'

'Now or later?'

'It's up to you . . . It's your tongue.'

'But it's your cunt.'

'Then do it now.'

I come several times, without any special effort. It's really good. And we're just getting started. We climb the small spiral staircase up to the bedroom. He quickly puts on a condom so he can make the most of my juices . . . then we adopt a very well-behaved missionary position.

'Ride me,' he says after a while.

First I straddle him, then, when he's completely inside me, I swivel around to face the other way. After a little while he pulls himself out and asks me to return the favour with my mouth. I suck him off until he comes, gently tugging at my long hair.

We barely have time to talk. Still using my mouth, I revive him. In a delirious sixty-nine, he starts playing with my arse. This turns me on. I can't help myself and climb on. Then, up to the hilt in my arsehole, he picks me up and sets me on all fours. In the end, he asks to come in my mouth again. I let him. The CD ends almost exactly at the same time as our second round. Game over. The end of the CD is the sign that his hour is up. If he wants to, he can have a bath, pay what we arranged on the phone and . . .

'See you later.'

No hard feelings. Life goes on. Job done, payment received (and discreetly checked, without his noticing, of course). He was the first client of the day. There are still five to go. With less than an hour and a shower between clients, I barely have time to get ready again. I prefer to do everything in one go, and meet my goal of five clients as soon as possible, so I can be free for the rest of the day. My system works. When I'm behind schedule or a client is late, the next one to arrive waits in the foyer downstairs. Until it's time to do it all again.

This ritual of running through a checklist of my body and room when the intercom rings is always the same. My second client is the really shy sort that you have to take by the hand. You have to lead him through the sex. It's mechanical. I'm unable to come with him because it's a tense shag – for both of us.

The third, a total kid, has the energy (and speed) to do me three times. It's his third visit and I've nicknamed him 'rabbit', although he doesn't know it. These quickies don't give me time to come. Never mind. We get along well and always talk a lot.

The fourth one brings his lover around for a threesome. A really interesting woman, who knows what she's doing. She isn't beautiful, but she turns me on. If his girlfriend and I don't control ourselves, he might end up empty-handed. Of course I'm not going to let that happen . . . She goes down on me, while he fucks me until I come. Not from the ride, but her tongue.

The fifth is the sort you'd take home to meet your parents. There's no chemistry, but we get along well. He is forty-something, and manages to do something I've never seen before. He comes without me even touching his dick, while I suck his balls. Ah, and he's brought me a lemon pie. Very nice. After riding him a little, our second round ends with him coming in my mouth.

The sixth and last of the day wants me to take him to a swingers' club. It's his first time. Yet another I'm about to lead astray . . .

It's been a while since I've worn a dress, so I choose one that is really only a piece of cloth. It has a plunging neckline and only just covers the essentials. I wear a pair of lace-up sandals. I want to be a knockout, and succeed, of course. I'm the sexiest girl at the Marrakesh tonight. But after a bit of drinking and dancing, my client still hasn't got into the spirit of the place.

'I don't feel relaxed in a room with so many people fucking.'

We go to the only room where unaccompanied men are allowed in. I sit on an empty sofa and he goes down on me. Then out of the blue, some guys show up. Two sit on the arms of the sofa and another two just stand there, watching. When my client notices them he gets a fright and we end up going to a private room, just the two of us. Since we have some chemistry going, I don't even worry about swapping partners. He doesn't want to either. We go for it all night long. Blow jobs, tit-fucking, rimming . . . Whenever I go to a swingers' club, I get excited at the possibility of swapping partners and getting it on with an interesting woman. My client is in luck because today there are only middle-aged women. Nothing against them – they just don't turn me on. Something almost happens with a guy of about forty who pulls me towards him, but he isn't accompanied. Although I don't get to go down on another woman or swap partners, the night is worth it. I get home at 5.30 a.m.

Wild sex, group sex, lots of different men (and women) every day, nights that never seem to end. What might seem exciting to many girls like me, in the full bloom of their twenties, is routine. It has been my daily grind for the last three years. Working five days a week, with an average of five clients a day – do the maths to work out how many times I've had sex for money. Much as I might enjoy myself, and have orgasms, it's still work. Work that I chose because I had no other choice when . . . Well, it's a long story. My personal story, and Bruna's. Yes, there are two. One girl – me – with two stories.

A stranger. I was dancing alone when a boy pulled me towards him and kissed me. My first night on the town. I didn't even ask his name. My first time out on my own at night. Freedom at the age of thirteen going on fourteen. I'd been there for less than half an hour. My first kiss. We went from kissing to groping one another, right there in the middle of the dance floor. Then, when I least expected it, he ditched me. Just like that, without any feelings, without a word. That night, I went with ten other boys. One wasn't enough. I needed lots to satisfy me. Raquel had woken up to sex.

A stranger. Although I was nervous, I used an introduction that I'd quickly rehearsed on the spot.

'I'm Bruna. I do oral, vaginal and anal.'

I finished by stating my false age, eighteen, not knowing that no one markets herself like that.

No one could know this was my first client. I'd left

my parents' house less than half an hour before to go to that new house. My debut at the age of seventeen. I wasn't going to tell that stranger I'd never had sex for money. He'd chosen me straight up. I wanted to disappear, make a run for it and go home to my parents. Instead, we went upstairs to the bedroom. I thought about my mother. The stranger touched me and wanted to have sex without a condom. She must be suffering, I thought. I didn't let him touch me. After sticking his finger into me, we had sex with a condom. All I could think was: I'm going to take this guy's money and go home. There's still time to give up and leave. I ended up having six clients that afternoon. I never went home again. I never saw my parents again. Bruna was born.

Little more than three years separate these two moments, so distant from one another. In the first, Raquel underwent a sea change, from sweet, spoilt daughter to lying teenager with no limits. I'd practised lots of kisses on the bathroom mirror, oranges, my arm, always following the tips I'd seen in teen magazines. The real thing had been even better. I'd found in my body, between my legs, the key to freedom and my bread-and-butter, even though it meant lying about my age and putting into practice, for 100 *reais* an hour, the little I'd learnt the six times I'd had sex with a serious boyfriend and another guy I'd gone with.

Each night I hit the dance floor at the Kripton, in the neighbourhood of Vila Olímpia, I wanted more and more. I wore short skirts to make things easier for anyone who wanted to feel with their hands what the almost-darkness concealed. If I didn't have sex there, if I didn't want to lose my virginity in the middle of the dance floor, it wasn't for lack of opportunity. The pleasure of feeling a boy get a hard-on because of me, rubbing and grinding against me through his trousers, was almost irresistible. Almost . . .

I unzipped lots of boys' trousers there on the dance floor, just so I could pull their underpants down a little and play with their dicks. I hadn't the slightest idea how to masturbate a man, until one of them asked me to in no uncertain terms. 'How 'bout a wank?' There was no way out, so I told the truth. 'I don't know how.' While I leaned against a wall, feeling silly and listening to his naughty laughter, he patiently took my hand and taught me the movement. From then on, I only didn't do it to those who didn't want me to. Making a guy come, giving him pleasure, was amazing. I started wanking off everyone I went with on the dance floor. No one around us noticed, because they were occupied doing exactly the same thing. I saw lots of couples having sex on the sofas. There was no problem with the bouncers. Whenever they caught a couple being a bit more daring or exhibitionist, they just asked them to tone it down.

I never had sex there. I had lots of opportunities, but lacked the courage. To lose my virginity, it would have to be with someone special. I'm romantic. Not that this stopped me from letting boys touch me more intimately. I'd pull my knickers down a bit under my miniskirt, and just their hands touching my thighs and between my legs would make me really wet. I thought that this was coming. Only later did I discover that 'getting there' was something else again – and better. I've learnt that coming, for me, starts with a chill in the stomach. Even so, I still didn't want to have sex.

I got really close to going all the way. Twice I got in a car with a guy and we took off our clothes. We did everything and I went as far as I could. And that was pretty far. But when it was time to do it, to have a guy inside me, I got cold feet.

'I've got to go.'

'Now that things're heating up?'

'Dad'll be here to pick me up soon.'

'He can wait,' he'd say, his dick already out of his trousers and his hands like two octopuses, with fingers all over me.

'I can't.'

'But you're almost naked, and we've done nearly everything. The only thing left is'

'Well, it's not happening. Sorry.'

I always made up an excuse and disappeared.

For the boy, who was older, I'd be just 'one more'. And I didn't want to be just 'one more'. I would have felt used. There was still a little reason left in my romantic head. Have sex in that place and never see the guy again? It wasn't my idea of what my first time should be like. Not to mention my fear of the pain and bleeding that teen magazines talked about. I thought I'd bleed a river of blood.

Truth be told, it was inexperience. Not wanting to confess that I was a virgin, and equally afraid to ask the guy to wear a condom, I imagined myself in the shoes of a friend who'd got pregnant at the age of fifteen. She didn't even know who the kid's father was.

'Mummy, who's my daddy?'

'I don't know, darling . . .'

I knew all too well what this kind of talk meant.

On my first day at the house on Alameda Franca, the last thing I wanted was for anyone to realise I didn't have any experience. I arrived at about two o'clock in the afternoon, after walking from Paraíso, where I lived, leaving behind everything I had:

15

mother, father, bedroom, clothes. I was carrying a file and a schoolbag packed with a few clothes and lots of bikinis to wear on my first job. I needn't have bothered. No one worked in bikinis . . .

I didn't have any decent clothes to work in, so the other girls found me some terrible things to wear. Me of all people – who'd always expressed herself through designer labels, which made up for my chubbiness and ugly-duckling syndrome. I had to accept the situation. I knew one day I'd have my own money and would buy all the designer stuff again.

The madam of the house on Alameda Franca, Larissa, was the only one I told part of the truth. She asked to see my ID, and I couldn't hide it: I was only seventeen.

'Don't tell anyone,' she advised me.

Much as I pretended to be experienced in front of the other girls, I gave myself away right from the start.

'What's your working name?' asked Larissa.

'Raquel,' I said naively.

'No working girl uses her real name. In this place, you're going to have to change it.'

'You look like a Bruna,' said Mari, who ended up becoming a good friend.

I don't remember why, when or how old I was, but I got it into my head that I was adopted. When I

16

was five, I asked my mum. When she confirmed it, I didn't have the guts to ask what adoption actually meant. I took my question to my teacher, who explained that people who were adopted had been abandoned as babies because their mothers couldn't or didn't want to bring them up. A couple would come along and choose one of these children for adoption. 'Choose?' I felt like an object. Although my parents had always treated me as a daughter, it was hard not to be angry, even if I kept it to myself. Kids came from their mothers' bellies, for Christ's sake. I only began to accept that that wasn't true much later. Perhaps too late.

I tried to accept things, because I really did have a family. But someone would always come along and say that I was very different from my older sisters and my mum. She is very European-looking, with fair skin and hair, dark eyes, and delicate features. The only thing we have in common is our height. She is as short as I am. Sometimes we even wore each other's clothes. But that was the end of our similarities. My two sisters, on the other hand, look exactly like my mum.

I even had an uncle who never treated me as a niece. For those who knew my dad, the excuse was 'She takes after him'. Never in a million years. He's six foot two, fat, white . . . Sometimes, to protect me from prejudice and aggression, Mum lied to strangers, inventing something to shield me. How I envied my friends who looked like their parents, like their real families! My anger passed from my biological to my adoptive parents. When we fought, I called them 'aunt' and 'uncle'. My poor mum . . . But I didn't have the maturity or inner resources to deal with it alone.

When I was seven, in 1991, we all went back to the city of Sorocaba, where we were originally from. That is, we moved to our country house in Araçoiaba da Serra. Dad had had an accident and had to stop working. One day, in the garage, he bent over to pick something up and when he stood up again he hit his head on a low ceiling-beam. I don't know how, but that blow seriously affected his brain. It was only when I saw him black out, in the middle of the living room, that I realised how serious it was. He couldn't continue working, at the height of his law career, and this crushed him. He went into a deep depression. It really was best for us to move to the country.

Although Dad's illness was a very tense, difficult phase, I can't complain. There were breathers: I played a lot, sometimes with Mum and occasionally even with Dad. He hung a basketball net in the garden between the fruit trees, and I'd spend hours practising, dreaming of one day playing professionally. With my height, that was to be yet another impossible dream . . .

To my mind, all the prostitutes in São Paulo were on Rua Augusta. I'd been there many times, even with my parents. Look at the pros, someone would always say. How does a woman get to that point? I used to think. I thought that was the only place where there were prostitutes, on that dirty, ugly street. Either there or in those old crumbling houses with heavily made-up women hanging out of the windows, calling to men passing in the street. Inside, all they had to do was spread their legs and wait for the client to come, and that was it. The so-called 'life'. Were call girls like that too? Not according to the newspaper ads. 'Girls between 18 and 25: earn at least 1,000 reais a week attending executives!'

The weeks before I ran away from home, when I'd already decided that that was what I was going to do, I bought newspapers for the classifieds and skived off school to visit a few of these places – clubs, brothels, massage parlours. I didn't see anything as shabby and run-down as on Rua Augusta, much less a bunch of women who'd gone to the dogs. Most places, like the Bahamas, were tasteful, really elegant. From the outside, you don't even realise what's inside. They impressed me. There was nothing abnormal about the girls I saw there. They didn't have 'pro' stamped across their foreheads, nor did they hang around in doorways offering themselves to passers-by.

The house on Alameda Franca, in the neighbourhood of Jardins, was the one I chose. I didn't know how to do anything. I had no experience and hadn't even finished secondary school. To leave home, I'd have to bite the bullet and give it a try – and earn those 1,000 *reais* for what I did. My prejudice disappeared and I said, 'That's what I'm going to have to be.' And I confess, I fantasised about having lots of men, and the idea started to grow on me. After all, I'd only had sex six times, very mechanically, and I'd never seen a porno film in my life. It was a chance to discover where sex could take me.

'That's it, open your legs nice and wide.'

'Like this?'

'Now let the doctor examine you to make sure everything's OK.'

First one finger, then another, which he pulls out and sniffs.

'Hummm, you've passed the medical.'

After my debut with the 'gynaecologist', my illusion that all you had to do was spread your legs crumbled. So did my fantasy of having lots

THE SCORPIONS SWEET VENOM

of different men, because I'd only considered *my* idea of men. But this 'shock treatment' was a good test to see if I really did want my independence.

It was hard going to bed with a stranger, even if he was a neatly dressed would-be gynaecologist. So imagine what it was like going upstairs with an enormous old Japanese man of about sixty. He was my second client. Never in my life had I imagined myself with a guy like that. But he picked me – and paid. To say no, I'd have to pay the house what the client would have paid. That was the agreement. I did my maths. To earn 100 *reais*, I had to have three clients. Be chosen, don't choose. It's no accident that lots of girls snort coke and smoke a lot of dope. I knew firsthand what that was all about. Snorting and smoking.

The Japanese guy started taking off his clothes, and I tried to focus on the money. I had an hour of him in front of me. He was older than my dad! All I could think about was trying to make him come fast to get it over and done with. We chatted a little. He couldn't get it up. I gave him a blow job, played with him, and nothing. I felt lots of different sensations, smells, things I didn't want to feel. I told myself I didn't feel a thing. He ran his hands over me. I didn't like it.

To this day, I sometimes feel sick when I see a

hand stroking my body. I do it to them, but I don't always like it in return. I only have sex listening to music, which helps me tune out, get on to another wavelength (besides which the CD lasts exactly one hour, which helps me keep track of time). Sometimes I imagine another man there, a boyfriend. And I look to one side, so I don't have to see the hand exploring my body, my private parts. It's all about chemistry. But I ploughed ahead and managed to give the Japanese a hard-on. I didn't know what was worse. I put a condom on him, got on top, rode him, let him fuck me and, of course, it wasn't good. It was more than mechanical. That day, I actually cried with another client; I told all of them it was my first day on the job.

People always give themselves something to make up for a bad day, a difficult week. It's no different for girls who make a living from sex. I deserve it! I thought. With the first money I managed to save from prostitution, I gave myself a mobile phone. I felt rewarded, somehow, for every time I'd ignored my nausea so as not to lose the client. It's funny, but I've never been turned off by anyone before getting into bed, no matter what they look like. It's only there, in bed. Not because of anything on the guy's body, a flaw or a scar (although I have my preferences). What gets me is the smell. Their body odours. Some men shower and it doesn't make any difference. Some also have bad breath. They're the worst ones. That's why kissing is such a sensitive issue. I don't kiss everyone. And not all of them want to kiss. The lonely ones are the kissers. Sometimes, even when I don't feel like it, I have to kiss them. It ends up being kind of lacklustre. I don't have much choice. It's part of the job. So I take a deep breath and off I go.

The little more than three years that we lived in the country were coming to an end. Dad had recovered considerably from the accident and they decided it was important for my education to go back to São Paulo. After all, I was going to start my fifth year of school in 1995. My oldest sister had already moved to Cajuru, near Ribeirão Preto, because of her work. My middle sister was living in our flat, so my parents bought a new one for us in the same neighbourhood. Everyone would have their own space. Very modern, considering my parents' upbringing – one daughter living in a country town and another living on her own. If it was true that the oldest kids paved the way for the younger ones, I had nothing to worry about.

As a result of the move, I had to leave behind a boxer dog, Lunna (my favourite), a Weimaraner, Fedra, and a mongrel, Paco. But the most important thing I left behind was a piece of my childhood, my happiness. Much as I loved São Paulo, going back became a trial. My parents were afraid of robberies, rape, everything. And they wouldn't let me out. For someone who'd run free, playing in the street or garden, being stuck in that flat in Paraíso was hell. I was eleven and wanted to explore the world. My friends started going to shopping centres and after-noon dance parties, and I couldn't. Since I had no freedom, I started lying so I could go wherever I wanted.

Mum was overly protective of me and showed it. I couldn't have a boyfriend, even if he was the most perfect guy in the world. Now Dad . . . He'd never played the role of father. OK, so he'd had the accident, his illness, he left his brilliant career right at the peak, and went into a huge depres-sion. I now know that his aggression towards me was the result of all the heavy-duty prescription drugs he had to take. While I used to blame him, I understand now that things weren't exactly as they seemed.

The so-called rebellious-teenager phase that the over-protection sparked off almost spiralled out of control, and fights, especially with Dad, became routine. I often thought about leaving home or looking for my biological parents to see if they wanted me back. If their reason for abandoning me was financial, it wouldn't be a problem. I'd work, pay my way. The only place where I might find a clue as to the whereabouts of my real parents was in Sorocaba, where I was born and adopted. But I couldn't quite bring myself to follow this up.

I studied at Bandeirantes, a very traditional and demanding school – so much so that even when I worked my backside off to get into the sixth year, I ended up in the bottom class. Those who study there know well what that means . . . Even so, my parents were proud of me. While on the one hand I wanted freedom, and lied a lot to get it, on the other, I had my own prejudices and insecurities. And I played the good daughter.

My middle sister, who is now thirty, started going out with a guy my parents didn't approve of. She was already living on her own. Well . . . let's say not all the time. My mother found out about this tiny detail. They put a lot of pressure on her to break up with the guy and she didn't think twice. She ran off with him. I saw how much this made my parents suffer. I couldn't remain indifferent. I was so angry with my sister. I prayed a lot for my parents. I think that was the only time in my life that I asked for something in a prayer, and it wasn't even for me. I always thank God for protecting me and that's it. I don't think God does anything for us besides pro-tect us. But I wanted Him to do something for my parents. Little did I imagine, torn between my anger with my sister and the desire to be free, that I was to replay this story myself.

When my sister's relationship ended (the guy's decision, by the looks of things), she returned home depressed, almost sick, going on about death and everything. My parents didn't pat her on the head and say, 'Darling daughter, we love you so much.' They made it clear that they wanted her to suffer for her own mistakes. They ignored her, refused to talk to her. And I followed their example, even though I really wanted to hug her and tell her everything would be all right.

I remember the day I saw my mother having a serious talk with her. I knew that expression. Mum would go red and her eyes would go dry – no sparkle in them whatsoever. She'd speak calmly, but in a strange tone of voice, leaving no doubt as to the seriousness of her words. Her forehead would crease up differently, showing wrinkles that only appeared when she was angry. It was worse than getting spanked – even though she'd never laid a finger on me. In the end, of course, they saw how serious it was and supported my sister. Off she went to the psychiatrist. It was exactly the same with me: why couldn't they talk to us? Why did our problems have to be resolved by strangers? I wanted to talk, but to them. Maybe they didn't know any other way to be. But I think I'll be different with my children.

I always thought that the first time for a girl was more important than for a boy. I was wrong. With every guy who loses his virginity to me, I become more and more convinced of this. OK, so in the future they probably won't even remember properly who it was (hard, in my case), but the sensation of being face to face with a woman, being able to touch her, hold her, a flesh-and-blood woman instead of a girlie maga-zine . . . Finally to discover the consistency of a breast, and learn how to touch it, run their hands around the cave of pleasures hidden between every woman's thighs. To be able to smell, lick her. Some of them – thirteen-, fourteen-year-olds – tremble at the sight of my naked body. I can almost read their thoughts. 'Can I touch them?' is what I hear them say most, wanting to feel my breasts. Their hands are generally cold. I sense a fear of failure in the air. A fear that I might compare their penises with others. Or a terror that they might come much too soon. I lead, teach and indulge. I feel special. In a way, I will always be remembered by every one of those boys – 'children' just like me. And there've been a lot.

Since Dante Alighieri School was close to the house I worked in, you can imagine how many lost their virginity down that way . . . The boys would come in groups. As minors were not allowed (although I worked there), they'd ring from a public phone to make sure the coast was clear and the police weren't about to turn up. They'd come in a huge group, although it was all very respectful, no messing around. It was like a school outing, the boys wearing blue tracksuit bottoms with a yellow stripe, and plain T-shirts with the name of the school on the front. Dressed like that, they looked even more childish. We'd leave the door of the house ajar and they'd come racing in. We all loved those boys. They didn't stir up trouble and spent well.

There I was, seventeen years old, going upstairs with boys of twelve, thirteen, fourteen. How strange – me, so inexperienced, in bed with someone even less experienced! But it ended up being natural. At that age, boys are in a bit of a rush. In the beginning it was strange, difficult even. But I got used to it. And I learnt how to make them relax and go all the way. 'Slowly.' 'Is it hurting?' 'Yeah, like this, look.' No manual's a substitute for a good teacher . . .

I was almost always the one they chose. After all, I didn't look that much older than the girls they'd already wanked off over, sighing with infatuation. I'd go upstairs with the boy. It was only when we got to the bedroom that some of them confessed.

'You won't tell my friends it's my first time, will you?'

'I don't have any reason to,' I'd reply.

I never laughed at any of them. Who am I to laugh at inexperience? I taught them how to touch my breasts, let them undress me, touch me, smell me, see close up what a woman's private parts were like. I taught them how to remove their first bra, the one no one forgets. I'd put on some music and put on my show. Some were brilliant students.

I liked to remove their uniforms slowly. It was easy to take off those tracksuit pants with a characteristic bulge in the crotch. I'd take hold of their rock-hard dicks, which sometimes accidentally came without me doing anything. The risk of this happening the first time was always high. So I'd suck them off to help them relax. I think they preferred blow jobs to actually fucking. They loved them. Horny little buggers, weren't they? I went down on a lot of these boys without condoms, just because they looked OK. I think I taught many of them very well. And the sex was almost always no-dramas. No acrobatics. The good old missionary position. They just wanted to get laid and have fun. The fantasies and variations come with time. It's a bit different with the more experienced ones.

*   *   *

I did everything I could to keep up my reputation as a 'little saint' with my parents. I'd come back from the dances and tell them I'd only danced. One night, however, I arrived home with dark love bites on my neck that I'd got from Thiago, a boy I'd gone with several times. We never became boyfriend and girlfriend because, when I saw him in the light, the beauty that the darkness had suggested wasn't the slightest bit evident. I also didn't want to hurt my lips any more with our kisses. The fact that we both wore braces was torture. But the crimson marks were there. There was no make-up that could cover it. And believe me, I tried.

Mum noticed, of course, and made me go to school the next day in a linen blouse that covered my neck. It was useless: I was really hot and it didn't cover the marks properly. But I wasn't ashamed. I didn't care that I had a reputation as a slut at school. It was as if I was a boy. For them, getting around was a sign of masculinity. For me, a love bite was a trophy, proof that someone had wanted me one night. A night of wild sex, who knows? I knew the truth. They didn't. That was what I loved about it. It was my way of getting everyone's attention. Me, a thirteen-year-old girl with a face covered in pimples, still a little on the chubby side, although I'd lost 20 kilos dieting. None of the boys at school paid me any attention, nor did anyone in the street, or anywhere. Only in the night. I must have looked beautiful in the dark. As Thiago had looked to me.

In my attempts to prove myself, I also started smoking in secret in the school toilets. I was a real sheep. I hung out with the tough kids. Many of them, at twelve and thirteen, already smoked dope. I didn't want to be labelled a square, but I was happy with my clove cigarettes for the time being. What was so great about taking a few tokes on a bit of weed rolled in fine paper while hiding in the alleys of Paraíso, near the school, while we skived off? Just to laugh at nothing and talk shit, say things that made no sense? I burnt my tongue when I lit up my first joint, when I was just fourteen.

At that age, no matter how grown-up we think we are, deep down we're not really all that sure about things. When I started smoking, for example, I didn't like the taste and the dizziness I felt. I didn't even know how to inhale properly – and that was hell for me. 'Look at Raquel – she doesn't know how to inhale . . .' Act like an idiot in front of the gang? I practised a lot until I was able to forget the bad taste and the cough. All to fit in, to be the same as my friends. Same? Friends? These 'friends' aren't around any more. But the bad habits are. And not just these ones.

With alcohol it was more or less the same. I didn't like the taste and didn't see what was so great about it. One day, to show that I was cool, I asked an older guy from school to buy me a can of beer, which I drank really quickly so I wouldn't have to taste it. I asked for another and another, also duly downed in a single gulp. After the third, everything was spinning. Although caught up in the euphoria and heat of the binge, I worried about getting caught by a plain-clothes school guard roaming the neighbourhood looking for students up to mischief.

All this effort to be cool, smoke, drink and party started to show in my school reports, which – when I didn't manage to intercept them from the mail with the help of the building janitor – mysteriously appeared in my mother's hands. There were the missed classes (which I always tried to justify by saying that the teacher hadn't heard my 'here' in roll call) and the marks that were getting worse by the day, which were more difficult to explain. None of this, however, stopped me from lying and getting up to no good.

Because of my bad behaviour, I couldn't afford to let my school marks drop. Since I skipped classes every day and couldn't understand a thing in my textbooks, I started cheating. Tests at Bandeirantes were printed on different-coloured paper for the different years. It was easy. I bought the same coloured paper as that used in the test, then copied everything I thought would be in the test on to it at home. It wasn't my idea; lots of Bandeirantes students did this. As usual, I followed the crowd. When the teacher wasn't looking, I'd shove the page into the test papers. It was perfect!

This tactic worked for me until the last test of the year – history. I only needed one point to get through, but I fell to temptation. And the teacher's wrath. Kicked out of class, on my way home, I was a bit stunned, scared about what Dad would say or do, and I almost got run over. I wish I had. When I got to my building I stalled before heading upstairs. I rang the doorbell. Dad opened the door. 'Hi there. How'd your test go?' I burst into tears. To my surprise, he hugged me. I cried even harder, ashamed. 'If I tell you, you're going to kill me.' I told him the truth, expecting to feel his hand come down on me. I don't know why; he'd never laid a finger on me. He just wanted to know why I'd done it and made me promise never to cheat again. That was not my only surprise, nor the only lesson I learnt from the episode.

When Mum was called into the school, my teacher told her it was normal for students to cheat. And that my cheat sheet was too big. Laughing, she held up the enormous sheet of paper. 'You'll have to learn to make smaller ones.' I couldn't believe it. I'd got a DIY lesson in cheating. She also praised me, saying she'd give me the point I needed to pass as I was a student who never stirred up trouble. Me? The things I got up to in her class — when I actually attended! Human generosity really walks strange paths.

We'd already been in the room for almost half an hour. Though fast, both first and second rounds had been good. We had another half-hour, but the guy wasn't showing any signs of wanting to go for it again. Lying next to me, both of us naked, he asked if he could snuggle up to me. He got comfortable in my arms and there he stayed, playing with my breasts with his fingers, running them up and down my tummy. He was the one who broke the silence.

'I'm attracted to my mother.'

I like to talk to my clients. I talk a lot and they end up opening up to me. The things I've heard . . . It's my psychologist side. I'd like to be a psychiatrist, but I know I'll never get into medical school. But there's always psychology, closely related. And that's what I'm going to do, when I go back to my studies. I'll never be at a lack for material. But that's not what I was talking about . . . I'd read *Oedipus*, that book about the guy who's attracted to his mother, Jocasta. But I'd considered it nothing more than a Greek tragedy until that point-blank confession. The guy and his frankness awoke my curiosity. We talked a lot and he told me his mother had fallen pregnant with him when she was very young, only sixteen. He must have been about forty-four, because, according to him, his mother was sixty.

His attraction stemmed from his childhood (how Freudian can you get?). When he was still very young, his mother used to go round the house in a bra and knickers, and was very relaxed about it. They bathed together and everything. This desire and fantasy had stayed with him all his life. Even today, at his age, the guy is obsessed with the idea of having sex with her. When we'd finished, he told me he'd give me whatever I wanted if I could get her to go to bed with him. I led him on and asked for 10,000 *reais*. I admit the money was tempting, but I hadn't the slightest idea how to convince her to sleep with her son. He told me how he imagined the sex would be, how he'd take off her clothes, smell her knickers, lick her all over, the positions. A thousand fantasies. Which remain in his head.

My desire to find out everything about life seemed boundless when I was fourteen. There were still things I wasn't clear about, of course. One of them was my own sexuality. I'd already given a lot of pleasure to the boys I'd masturbated at clubs, I'd held a lot of stiff dicks, but I didn't know if that was as far as pleasure went. I was curious to know what it was like to come into contact with another woman's body. And I was also afraid. What if I was a lesbian? At that stage in life, things are either black or white. If something's not black, it must be white. But I tried not to give it too much thought.

One day, at school, the boy who sat in front of me had a copy of *Playboy*. He started flicking through the magazine in the middle of the lesson, and I peered over his shoulder like a pirate's parrot, fascinated by what I saw. I'd never seen magazines of naked women. These things never came into my house. Imagine the embarrassment of buying one at a newsstand. I asked to see it. He lent it to me and I loved it. During the break, I didn't think twice. I stole the boy's *Playboy*, stuffed it in my bag and took it home. I'd already masturbated looking at *G Maga-zine* – which I'd bought often. But I'd never come looking at those guys with their hard-ons. Perhaps I'd finally come if I looked at women. Bingo! After this feat my fantasy had to leave the page and become reality.

I went to a party with a friend – a really good friend – and arranged to sleep at her house after-wards. We drank champagne until we couldn't drink any more, and got really smashed. Back at her place, she decided to take a shower.

'Come on, you're taking ages in there.'

'I can't hear you.'

I went into the bathroom to harass her.

'I want to have a shower too.'

'So come in then,' she answered innocently, with no ulterior motives. So I did . . .

I remember the sensation of torpor and pleasure at being there, face to face with another girl, naked, showering in front of me.

'What's wrong?'

'Nothing.'

My excitement was mounting, but I didn't make the first move. In spite of my confusion, my lust, desire, availability, fear, I found it all odd. I just stared. It all passed, however, when she took the initiative. Under the hot shower, the bathroom filled with steam, the two of us silent, wet, she delicately ran her hands over my body. I let myself go with each touch. I touched her too and got another touch in return. A body just like mine. Her sex just like mine. Feminine, curvaceous, soft. We slept together that night and it was really good.

It never happened again with her. We both felt embarrassed. Neither of us said a word about that night either. And our friendship cooled off. How could I share things with a friend I'd been to bed with? We met up some time later and became friends again, but it was never the same. I regret what we did that night. No matter how good the experience was, I'd rather have my friend back.

One day, two clients turned up together.

'Do you want to go one at a time?'

'We want to go at the same time.'

Wow! Was I up to it? I'd never done a double penetration before (the so-called DP). They say curiosity killed the cat. In my case, the cat has seven lives and is still going strong.

'Let's do it!'

In the beginning, I didn't know who to pay attention to. I started by sucking one off, but the other came and knelt next to his friend, so I gave them a double blow job. I kissed one, then the other. I wondered if something might happen between them, as it often does with women in a *ménage à trois*. But I realised nothing was going to happen between these two. Only the heads of their dicks touched, and even then only when I held them together and tried to suck them both at the same time. A difficult mission . . . although not impossible.

Having two men at my beck and call gave me an incredible feeling of power. One of them lay down and I got on all fours and started blowing him. The other one got behind me and rammed his dick into my cunt. After ages in this position, he decided to use the back door. The one I was blowing slid under me and slipped his dick in the front door . . . I could feel the two of them battling it out inside me. And they weren't exactly small.

'Can you feel the sword-fight inside you?'

'What a fight . . .'

It didn't matter that my movement was more restricted. Even better – everything can be done to a different rhythm. I discovered that I loved DP. The one behind me came first and left the room. I kept going with the other one for ages with me riding him, until he came. It was only after it was over that I saw that the first one's load had dripped on to the sheet. What a pain . . .

The day-to-day life of a working girl has a very unglamorous side. I shared my tidy but simple room – beds, large wardrobe, mirrors, impersonal pictures on the wall, like the ones you see in hotels – with four other girls. Nothing like what you see in the cinema, for example, with those dressing tables dripping with costume jewellery. Since we also worked there, we had to keep it clean. We took turns sweeping and dusting. Not all of them liked the housework, but letting the place get dirty wasn't an option . . . Washing the linen and clients' towels was the launderette's job. But the girls had to change them, otherwise they got revolting. Except that (don't tell) it wasn't one sheet per client. Sometimes it was the same one all day long, where several men had been. Smooth out the creases and *voilà*. I was always asking if I could change the sheets. Since there weren't that many, and she didn't want spend much at the launderette, the manager used to get angry and say no. Sometimes I'd spread gel on the sheet on purpose so she'd have no choice. She used to tell me off, of course. But I didn't care.

The first time I moved houses was about seven months after I started working. Actually, the madam of the house on Alameda Franca kicked me out, together with two other girls, because someone had told her we were smoking dope in secret. Although I'd met some really nice girls, with stories very similar to mine, there was a lot of jealousy. After all, the girls are competition for one another. That was why I'd never wanted to work in places like Café Photo or Bahamas. Just think! If it was like that with just ten girls at the brothel, imagine a hundred! I also don't like the idea of having to solicit clients. Either they want me and come to have sex, or I'm not interested. Since the most important thing in this profession is your body, there's a lot of bitching between the girls. It's not easy to make real friends in this business. I've never worked in a company, but I imagine it must be the same . . . So when you're chosen by the client, you'd better beware, because this is when the lid comes off. On one such occasion, a backstabber decided to let the cat out of the bag about the dope to make life hard for me. It worked.

I ended up going to a yellow house on Alameda Jurupis, close to Ibirapuera Shopping Centre. I had to keep working. It only lasted a few months because of a twist of fate. Mari called me one day saying that lots of clients were walking out of the Franca house because I wasn't there any more. As a result, the madam, Larissa, had to swallow a bit of pride and ask me back. I liked the house and went back, but only to work, since I'd rented a flat for myself on Avenida Miruna, in Moema. Although I'd blown a lot of money on alcohol, dope and coke, I already had some savings from the house on Alameda Franca, before they kicked me out. Since no bank would let me open an account (try doing this when you're an eighteen-year-old prostitute, with no recognised profession or fixed address, except the brothel), I went around with my money in a little bag, always worrying about it. I rented the flat more to have a place to hide my savings – and slept there because I'd already paid for it.

My return to the Franca house wasn't what I'd expected. The girls I knew were no longer there and it was all very strange. I needed action, something new, a horizon. I was also depressed, a bit lost and really wanted to give up coke. I knew that, if I didn't get my act together, I'd completely lose myself, with no objectives, just fucking all day long so I could snort and smoke after work. In other words – the image of a sorry, worn-out pro who ends up alone on a street corner or hanging out the window of an old house. I was determined to save enough money to be independent, without having to support some pimp. So I'd have to work more. A girl who lived in my building told me about the 'Big Twenty'. A pat on the back for whoever figures out the name. I was really curious to know how a girl could sell herself for 20 *reais*. If it was about quantity and high turnover, I was all for it.

She took me to a place in Campo Belo. It had a high client turnaround, lots of tiny individual rooms, zero luxury – and hygiene. A squalid, filthy fleapit. Imagine a room so small that the only things that fit in it are a rickety chair and a single mattress on the floor with a disgusting sheet on it (that's only changed once a day). It's a quick fuck, ten or fifteen minutes. Express sessions, 10 *reais* to the pimp, 10 to the girl.

I really wanted to see what the clients were like. There was every walk of life there – street sweepers, cleaners, guys that earned the minimum wage. Guys looking for a quick fuck, nothing else. But to my surprise, there were rich kids and executive sorts, too. One of my clients was an engineer in his forties who liked to fuck hard and really gave it to me. I was curious and couldn't contain myself.

'Why do you come here if you could go somewhere better?'

'I prefer it like this, rather than a long session once a week. That's why I come here every day.'

I developed more admiration for practicality after I heard this answer. I only spent two days at the 'Big Twenty.' But they were two highly educational days, I have to admit.

I really screwed things up at Bandeirantes in October 1999. I was fifteen. This time there was no turning back. There was nothing I could do. I had the hots for a guy in my class. Good-looking, blond, white skin, he looked like an angel, with really blue eyes. But he was so sleazy and full of himself that it spoilt everything. Until the day he came on to me.

During a class in the physics lab, the teacher turned out the light. We were all standing around the experiment. He stood really close to me. Suddenly, very gently, he took my hand. With my heart beating wildly, I let him. He guided my hand to his penis. I held him through his trousers. He was hard. I imagined everyone could hear my wildly beating heart. But fear spoke louder and I took my hand away. He didn't give up. He stood behind me and started rubbing up against me right there, in the middle of the lesson. I couldn't resist: he was coming on to me! Raquel, the chubby one! I was completely wet, excited and scared. I don't know how long we stayed there like that, with him rubbing his hard-on against me from behind, provoking me, turning me on.

Since it was the last class of the day, and it was already getting dark, he offered to walk me home. Actually, he wanted to convince me to go somewhere to do what we hadn't managed to finish in the class.

'It's late and Mum's going to tell me off.'

'Tell her you went to study anatomy with a friend from school.'

'Let's leave it for another day.' I played a little hard to get. Until he finally managed to twist my arm.

'C'mon, you're not leaving me like this, are you? I know you want it too.'

We stopped next to the wall of a school one street away from my place. I didn't let him kiss me, but I ended up wanking him off there in the middle of the deserted street, even though I wasn't really in the mood.

The next day during the class he kept on insisting and sending notes and I gave in. The time had come for me. After the class, a new adventure. Along the way, he stopped to buy condoms. I started to panic, as I had all the other times I'd almost had sex. I didn't want my first time to be like that. Nor did I want him to know I was a virgin. We stopped in a dead-end road.

'It's not going to happen.'

'What?'

'I told Mum I'd go out with her.'

'No way. We're here now and we're not going to just forget about it.'

I tried to leave again, but he didn't let me.

'You're not escaping without at least giving me a blow job.'

There was nothing else I could do. I'd only get out of there if I sucked him off. I couldn't say I didn't know how. How embarrassing! I'd never put a dick in my mouth and didn't have the slightest idea what to do. I imagined myself sucking an ice-lolly. I squatted on the ground while he leaned against the wall with his trousers down, holding my hair, controlling the rhythm. I didn't like the way he kept pushing my head. I held his dick at the base, near his balls. If I'd let him, he would have rammed the whole thing in. I was afraid of choking, but very excited. By the situation, his taste, his smell, the act itself, the fear of getting caught. Before long he started moaning, panting, shoving his dick forcefully between my lips. Then, a stronger shove, and I tasted something strange in my throat. He'd come in my mouth. But I didn't have the courage to swallow.

I don't know if it's true, but he told me it was the best blow job he'd ever had. So I made my debut with critical praise . . . All I know is that he really moaned as if he liked it. Once again I didn't have the courage to say that it was my first time. We promised to keep it to ourselves.

I was really silly and broke the promise myself. I told a 'friend', who worshipped the guy. And by the look of things, he didn't keep his mouth shut either. The gossip spread throughout our entire year in a matter of days. No one came to ask me if it was true, to hear my side of the story. I just heard the laughter and felt people staring at me. Some with malice. Others with disgust.

As if with the wave of a magic wand, everyone disappeared. Not even my 'friends' stood by me. I ended up completely alone. People were ashamed to be seen with me. One girl came to ask me how much I charged. I said nothing. Big mistake. I felt hard done by. Even the girls who were no longer virgins helped make and spread my reputation as a slut around the school. But I kept it together. I went to school as if nothing had happened and even though I felt alone and hurt. I shed few tears over it, although I was really suffering. I was only fifteen!

Then one day I'd had a gutful of the hypocrisy and said, 'I did it, I liked it and I'd do it again.' That shut a few people up. I knew I hadn't committed a crime. Then I realised something else. What exactly had the boy told people? Guys have this stupid, childish habit of blowing everything out of proportion, bragging. I never found out if that was what happened, since no one spoke to me. Not even him. But I think he must have made out that he'd had sex with me.

The story ended up in the head's office, of course. I denied everything and would have continued to my last breath. That day, I crumbled. I arrived home crying and told my mother everything. Well, not everything. I told her I'd left the school grounds to kiss a boy and that people were saying I'd had sex with him, that I'd performed oral sex on him.

It was the end of my eighth year of school and Mum thought it was better to change schools. I don't know if she believed me or was just pretending, like me. Bandeirantes was about to become history. That is, if another boy hadn't also left Bandeirantes and gone to study at Maria Imaculada – and ended up in the same class as me. The story was duly spread and once again Raquel was marginalised. Know what? Fuck them!

The 'Big Twenty' experience had really been very interesting. But it wasn't for me. I work with my body and, of course, I get tired. It isn't an easy life. Ten clients a day is bordering on insanity. Everything hurts. I had to try a different house, catch my breath and start again. But with a different mind. I ended up in a house on Rua Michigan, in Brooklin. Now I know why I had to spend some time there: it was where I earned my name. I've always loved the ocean. One of my sisters had a holiday flat in Guarujá, on the coast, and I used to go there a lot. Good times . . . My only moments alone were in the sea, without anyone else around. I even went body-boarding and surfing at some of the beaches there. But no one knew that.

There were two Brunas working at the house. A client asked for Bruna and the manager took him the other one.

'Not this one,' he said. 'I want the little surfer girl.'

I liked the guy. We had chemistry and got along well.

'Why did you call me a surfer girl?'

'You look like one.'

'Good, I like it!'

When I left this house and started working in my flat, I had to come up with a working name that suited me. I remembered the episode and didn't think twice. I'd be Bruna, the Surfer Girl.

*　　*　　*

48

I've already mentioned that one of the things that most irritated me about the brothels was the issue of the linen. Well here's another behind-the-scenes story. In the house on Rua Michigan, the girls had to wash the towels themselves (the bed linen went to the launderette). There were four washing machines and a bunch of clotheslines to dry them on. Except that when winter came and business picked up, the sun didn't come out and the dratted towels just wouldn't get dry. There was a heater in the room where we sat and waited for clients. We'd come downstairs after each client with the towel, and the manager would hang it in front of the heater, let it dry a little, check for stains and wrap it up again. Looks brand new, right? Several men would dry themselves with the same towel. Gross . . .

All the confusion, discovering sexual desire, gossip, losing my friends, and the fact that I'd always been chubby, sent me into a painful spiral. I fell into a depression and ended up on Prozac and the lot. And with all this going on, my fear of getting fat again led me to bulimia. I'd stuff my face with sweets, then stick my fingers down my throat and . . . it became a compulsion. I was hungry and ate a lot, I think because of the medication and my anxiety, then I'd rush away from the dining table to bring it all up again. On my way home from school, I'd stop and buy twenty *reais*' worth of sweets and chocolates every single day. I'd wolf them down practically all at once, just for the taste, then get rid of them a few minutes later. My mother caught on, probably because of the sound of the toilet flushing after every meal and the way I'd rush off. I took to vomiting in a newspaper so I wouldn't have to flush the toilet.

Who knows why I went into such a bad depression. Well, actually, I do know. I thought I was fat and ugly, I was adopted, and I had problems with my dad . . . As if that weren't enough, when I turned sixteen, after the fuck-up at Bandeirantes and the fact that the story had also spread to Maria Imaculada, I found myself with no friends. It got to a point where I couldn't see any way out. I decided to kill myself. It'd have to be something quick, where I wouldn't feel any pain or run the risk of staying alive, but quadriplegic, for example. A gun would be the best way. Dad had one at home. Legal, of course. Not that he'd ever used it; it was from the days when we'd lived in the country. I knew where he kept it.

One day, alone at home, I really hit rock bottom. I got the gun from its hiding place and, although I was shaking, stuck the barrel in my mouth. It's strange holding a gun. It's cold and its weight doesn't seem to match its size. It was as if I was holding something from another planet, a place that might well be my final destiny after firing the first and last shot of my life. I closed my eyes and got ready to pull the trigger with my thumb. There was this ridiculous pressure inside me, my head, my chest. I counted to three and . . . CLICK! The fucking thing wasn't loaded. Even so, I decided I still wanted to go through with it. I turned the place upside down and found the bag Dad kept the bullets in. I don't know what happened to me, but I was unable to load a single bullet in the revolver. I decided to give up. For the time being.

A week went past and I was still really bad. I took Prozac to stay awake and something else to get to sleep. I don't think either of them had the desired effect, because I spent seven nights in a row going over my life, seeing just how much I had to work out. I decided to try again. I waited for everyone to go to bed, placed a chair by the living-room window, which was the only one that didn't have bars on it, and figured that falling from the ninth floor would be fatal, which was my intention. I climbed up, stuck a leg out the window and, with half my body inside and the other half hanging out, I thought about all the bad things in my life. That would give me the strength to jump. But I couldn't think of anything bad enough to make me do it. Only good things came to mind: my dreams, the desire to make peace with my parents. My courage, which was already dwindling, threw itself out of the window before I could. I never tried again. I wanted to live. So, I'd have to do something for myself.

I'd already had two boyfriends, one at Bandeirantes and the other at Maria Imaculada, without ever having gone beyond a bit of heavy petting and oral sex. You'll think I'm lying, but I was still technically a virgin at the age of seventeen! In other words, no guy had ever had his dick in me. Which, technically speaking, is what qualifies a girl as a virgin. Honestly, I have no reason to lie about this now.

Since Mum kept a tight rein on me, and I didn't want my first time to be up against a wall in a dark alley or on a dance floor, it was hard fulfilling all of the requirements. Of course, I also had to be truly in love. I dreamt of finding a boyfriend and going to live with him, regardless of my age.

I found my third boyfriend on the Internet. At home, Dad and I both had our own computers, which ensured me a certain amount of privacy, even if only in the virtual world. I'd always been crazy about the Internet and spent hours surfing, writing and, of course, flirting on-line. Until the day I fell in love with a boy through the computer screen. It's true. We arranged to meet. Face to face, I thought he was horrible. If we hadn't been in love . . . We started going out for real.

At home, we suffered a lot of prejudice because he was a delivery boy. Daddy's little girl, middle class, going out with a guy like that? Dad refused to accept it. 'I don't want you going out with a poor guy, a delivery boy. Imagine if you married a guy like that – he wouldn't be able to support you. You'd have to work.' In his mind, all families were like his. Mum had never worked after getting married, although she had a degree in Language and Literature and had worked as a teacher for a while in Sorocaba before she married my father. The poor thing – how boring watching TV all day long, looking after the flat and her daughters, chatting on the phone.

Love is blind, deaf and mindless. But mute, never. I fought with my parents every day. I think that's why I did everything in my power to put an end to my virginity. Imagine the juggling act. My parents were away and my sisters didn't live with us any more. Whenever Mum was away, she asked the maid to stay the night – in the living room, to be specific. The maid always went to bed early, which made things easier.

I planned everything. My boyfriend arrived at the building and called me from his mobile. Without raising any suspicions, I said I was going to a girlfriend's place. I went downstairs to meet him and we took the service lift back up so we wouldn't have to buzz the intercom. When we got to my floor, he hid on the stairs. It was really exciting. Like something out of a film.

My heart was beating wildly; I was scared that something might go wrong. Then I ordered a take-away. When the food arrived, I asked the maid to go downstairs to get it. It was enough time for him to sneak in through the kitchen door and hide in the cupboard in my bedroom, while I behaved as if everything was normal in the living room. I got the food, left some for the maid to eat alone and locked myself in my room. He came out (no pun intended) and had dinner with me. We waited until we heard the maid snoring. With a full stomach, she quickly fell asleep. Then we left my room and, taking care not to wake her, headed for my parents' bedroom. It had to be on a double bed, of course . . .

It didn't really work the first two nights (of the five) that we repeated this scheme. It was only on the third night that I worked up the courage to have sex. It was crazy, awful, because it had been planned. It was really mechanical. I felt my hymen tear and that was that. All said and done, I'd only lost my virginity. No, that wasn't sex. It hurt a lot, and I couldn't scream or make a noise. It was a while before I got to have real sex. Was it worth it? Yes. I'd imagined that becoming someone's 'woman', completely, would be yet another reason for me to decide to leave home to live with him. But I realised that I didn't need to marry someone for that to happen. And I had to do something about it fast.

My breasts were small, in proportion to my body. I was happy with them, but it wasn't really about me. So off I went with my savings to get a boob job. And it wasn't just my tits that got bigger. There was a new 'dish' on Bruna the Surfer Girl's menu: oral, vaginal, anal and . . . tit-fucking! If you still haven't worked out what that is, I'll tell you. I squeeze my breasts together, creating a generic vagina in the soft region in between. In the beginning I thought it was funny, because it was as if I was watching someone have sex from the inside, with the head of the guy's penis appearing and disappearing, close to my mouth. I was even able to give the better-hung 'two-in-one', with a few licks on the head of their dicks when they got close. I've had clients who could only come that way.

I'd been working for almost a year when my first couple (in a long line of them) turned up at the house on Michigan. That is, my first pair. They were both married – but not to each other. They arrived and I eyed the woman curiously. I admit I got very excited. Going down on another girl while a guy goes down on you is indescribable. I came effortlessly. She returned the favour and went down on me with gusto. While she did this, I sucked him off. I was enjoying being the centre of attention. He fucked me lying down, while she offered herself to me, licked my nipples, and ran her tongue all over me. We kissed, caressed and went down on one another. If it weren't for me, the poor guy would have had to wank himself. I came twice.

This was the first time we'd had sex, and I thought it odd that she'd been more interested in me than in him. Nothing against it, but it just didn't seem natural. If I hadn't paid the guy any attention, it would have been as if he weren't there. I realised that she was turned off by him and avoided his efforts to please her, his touch, his attempts to kiss her, to go down on her. While he was showering, I started chatting to her. She was only interested in him for his money, and not for sexual pleasure. Her husband didn't make enough money to give her half of what her lover did. Brand-new car, jewellery – the kind of presents lovers give.

They could only meet once a week, for two hours. To free herself of the chore of having sex with him, she started demanding another woman in bed with them. She told him she liked it (and she really did seem to). It made the time go faster during their encounters, she said.

This woman was definitely an exception. After going out with couples became routine, and I'd been initiated into the interesting world of swingers' clubs, I came to a conclusion about women: they like being with other women. This story about 'indulging her husband's fantasies' is for a minority. It's a useful excuse. Women are shyer, more reserved, afraid of taboos. Of course there are situations where it's clear that it's the husband's doing, insisting his wife sleep with another woman. When they arrive they're afraid, frozen, don't know what to do.

Once I was in the uncomfortable situation of having a woman cry in front of me because she felt jealous seeing her husband with me. But then there are others who even encourage it. These women swear that they do it so their husbands won't cheat on them, because they're always together in their sexual adventures. If only they knew how many of them came back alone later . . . Not to mention those who've already come before. How many times have I heard them say, 'When she comes, you pretend you've never seen me before in your life, right?' I feel sorry for these women. They're having the wool pulled over their eyes and don't know it. Or they pretend not to know, not to notice, who knows. I'll never fall into the trap of trying to be liberal to avoid betrayal. Total satisfaction does not exist, nor does anything come with a guarantee.

It's funny – the reasons why these women actually come to share their beds and husbands with someone else are so many: fear, pleasure, jealousy, curiosity, insecurity, fantasy. But deep down, I believe that all women really like being with other women. Whether men enjoy being with other men, I'm not sure, because when I'm with two at the same time, even at 'parties' with DP and the whole works, I've never seen anything happen between them (which is a shame). If they do it when they're alone, well, that's another story . . . I've shared the intimacy of sex with lots of people, men and women, and I know what I'm talking about. I'm going to be an excellent psychologist, mark my words.

The delivery-boy boyfriend, the lies I told to get what I wanted, the trouble I got into and my grades at school – all this made my relationship with Dad go downhill. He tried to fix things: I failed my first year of secondary school and when I finally passed, he sent me to São Luís to see if a new environment would help. It didn't make any difference. I still couldn't be bothered studying.

Dad and I had terrible fights, but he'd never hit me, no matter how afraid I was that he might. Deep down, I always thought I deserved it. So I'm going to tell you the real story of why he hit me for the first time. I've never told anyone before out of sheer shame. I used to steal. No, I'm not a professional thief. It started when I was about eight and we lived in Araçoiaba. The local grocery shop had a sweet jar on the counter. As there was only one shop assistant, who was busy with Mum, it was easy to take the sweets on the sly – and I also savoured them on the sly. I knew all I had to do was ask and Mum would have bought me as many as I wanted. But the exciting part was the adrenalin, the fear of what was forbidden and the risk of getting caught. I only slipped up once and Mum asked where the sweets had come from. I lied. 'I got them at school.' It wasn't long before I discovered other facets of this uncontrollable urge. The sweets weren't enough and I discovered a compulsion for money. That's right – money has always held sway over me. Imagine – there I was, eight years old, stealing money from my parents! Since my father could barely leave the house due to his illness, there was always money at home. That was before the currency changed to the *real*. I didn't have the slightest idea what the money was worth. All I knew was that asking for it (and my requests would no doubt be met) was less exciting than taking it. I started taking a few notes every now and then from Dad's stash. Then I'd go into a shop and ask the assistant what I could buy with it. Even so, I continued stealing things from other places. Especially sweets.

We had a driver just to take me to and from school, which was in Sorocaba, since my father couldn't take me and my mother didn't like driving there. Along the way, I'd always ask him to stop at the Real, a wonderful bakery, saying my mother had asked me to buy something. I had the money in my purse and wouldn't even necessarily be in the mood for sweets or chocolate. I did this for a long time, until . . .

I don't know why, but Mum decided to take me to school one day. She stopped at the bakery and asked me to go in to buy something. When I came back, she came out with a really strange story: she'd seen the store security guards hauling a girl off to the office. And she said the security cameras had filmed the girl stealing things from the bakery. I had no idea these things even existed. To this day, I don't know if she knew something (which was quite possible, since everyone there knew her and must have tipped her off) and chose this way to give me a fright, or if it was a true story. All I know is that I stopped stealing outside our home. But only outside. Inside, it was always cash.

Even after we'd moved back to São Paulo, I'd take at least 50 *reais* a day. I did it for the excitement of doing something I shouldn't, because after all, my parents gave me an allowance and, if I needed more, all I had to do was ask. I became so addicted that I didn't let a single day go by without taking money. My mother caught me twice, and her pardon (which I begged for while bawling my eyes out, with real tears and shame) was like an open visa to continue doing it. On a couple of occasions she even mentioned to my father, in front of me, that money was disappearing from her wallet – I think in the hope that I'd come to my senses and stop. Sweet illusion . . .

I started stealing at school too. It was only 10 *reais* here and there, nothing much. No one took more than that to school. I'd wait for everyone to leave the classroom during the break, then go back in and rummage through people's bags. Until the day a girl left 30 *reais* on her desk and I didn't think twice. I swiped it without batting an eyelid. I ended up in the head's office . . . Someone had seen me going back into the classroom during break and grassed. When the head asked me if I'd done it, I didn't try to lie, and owned up. 'Yes, it was me.' She asked if I was taking drugs. It would have been silly to admit it, since I didn't spend everything I stole on weed. So I decided to lie. The punishment was to return the money. Guess what I did? I stole it from home. Case closed, or so they thought. But do you think money stopped disappearing from school? The other times, however, I took the blame but not the gain.

I'd really thought that if I returned the money, everything would be OK. But the head decided to call Mum in and tell her everything. She was devastated, and furious with me. We had a huge fight. But at that stage in the game, no matter how hard I tried to stop (and I did), I couldn't. I had to take more and more in order to feed another addiction – compulsive shopping. The things I bought were useless, but I had a crazy need to buy them. And this required more and more money.

I was so out of control that even the US dollars my sister had set aside (left over from a trip to the United States) shared the same fate. Before going back there to get married, she'd decided to renovate her flat and had taken the money to our parents' place to keep it out of reach of the workmen. I kept taking dollar bills until, before I knew it, I'd taken the lot. And it didn't stop. I started selling my books at second-hand bookshops until they were all gone. Then I took others from home. Enough! I promised myself I wouldn't do it any more. When I make a promise, I keep it. This time it didn't work.

One day when no one was at home, I went rummaging through drawers looking for money. I found a recorder and some of those little cassette tapes. I started listening and discovered that my phone calls had all been recorded. OK, so I'd screwed up a lot, but that was too invasive.

At the start of 2002, I thought: If I take lots of money and buy everything I want, then I'll stop. I remembered some Vivara jewellery that Dad had given Mum for their wedding anniversary the year before, which she'd never worn. I tried to sell the ring by itself, but no one wanted to pay more than 50 *reais* for it, even though the stone was rare. I temporarily gave up on the idea, until, one day, on an impulse, I decided to take the case with the whole set. I'd heard of a place on Oscar Freire that bought jewellery and paid well. I took everything with me to school in my bag. I'd actually forgotten it was there when a friend asked me for something and I told her to get it from my bag. There was a huge commotion. The girl made such a big scandal that the class stopped and even the teacher came over to see what was going on. The teacher asked why I was carrying the jewellery around and once again I lied, saying it was a present from my boyfriend that I was going to lend to a friend to wear to a party.

After the class, off I went to the store on Oscar Freire. The guy recognised the value of the jewellery but told me he could only pay 500 *reais*. I said no, of course. I took the case home and hid it in the cupboard again, although the thought of having 500 *reais* was really tempting. That was a lot of money for a seventeen-year-old girl. I thought about all the things I could buy and was unable to resist. My mother had never used that jewellery and wouldn't even notice it was missing. The next day I closed the deal. I took a taxi and immediately started to regret what I'd done. I asked the driver to go around the block and I went back to the store. Guess how much he was asking for me to buy it all back? Two thousand, five hundred *reais*!!! Where was I going to come up with that kind of money? I gave up. What was done was done.

In May, my mother decided to wear the jewellery to a wedding. Obviously, she couldn't find it. She even asked me if I'd seen it, and I lied, of course. She searched the whole house for that dratted jewellery and ended up wearing another set. I was relieved, at least temporarily. The next day was a Saturday and she turned the house upside down. I swear I wanted to tell her everything, but I didn't know how. 'It was the maid!' she concluded. I felt really guilty, because the maid had worked for my family for almost twenty years and I didn't think it was fair for her to get the blame for it. But I kept my mouth shut.

The next day, my mother arrived home saying she'd been to my school and that the head had told her I'd been behaving strangely, giving presents to my friends (I'd only been giving away my collections of stickers and writing paper). But the big revelation was that the story about the jewellery in the classroom had reached her ears. 'If it was you, I want it back,' she said, thinking I still had it. There was nothing I could do and I confessed everything, including that I'd sold it. She wanted to know how much I'd sold it for, but I didn't tell her. She freaked out, although she promised not to tell my father, for fear of his reaction or that he might have a stroke – since he was probably still paying off the present – or even beat me.

Some time went by, then one day I arrived home and saw my mother with that terrible expression on her face that only she knows how to make when she's angry. All she said was, 'I couldn't help myself and I told your father.' At that very moment I saw him coming towards me from the living room. Without a word, he started beating me. With his fist, his palm, every way possible. I don't know how, but people started arriving: my sisters, their friends, my brother-in-law. An audience formed. Dad dragged me to the sofa and continued hitting me. When he tired, I begged him to hit me more. Since I hadn't managed to kill myself, here was my chance.

'Go ahead and kill me. I'll let you kill me.'

'I'll kill you all right,' he said. 'I'm going to beat you to death.'

I decided to stand up to him. I didn't shed a single tear. I wanted to appear strong, no matter how much I was hurting. Dad said he'd already spoken to a couple of friends of his who were judges and that I'd be going straight to the juvenile detention centre. He beat me until they left to report me to the police.

My sisters gave me a tongue-lashing, of course. They 'reminded' me that I'd been adopted out of love and that I had everything they'd never had, because my parents hadn't always had money. But I back-chatted everyone, I'm not even sure why. When they got back, Dad continued beating me until he was tired. I went to bed in the clothes I was wearing, without even taking a shower. He came into my room, slapped me across the face and said, 'Here's one more.' This went on for three days, until he stopped hitting me. I was never left to my own devices again. There was always someone watching me, at home, in the street, on the way to school. At night, they locked the flat's two doors and went to bed. During the day, they locked the doors to the office and their bedroom, for fear I might steal something else.

A week later, Dad came to me and said, 'Today is your hearing.' Since he hadn't killed me, the juvenile detention centre had to be better. He and Mum went by taxi. I was given a metro ticket and instructions on how to get there. Along the way, I thought about running away, but I was scared and decided to face the judge. When I got there, we waited in a room with lots of mothers of kids who were locked away, because it was the hearing day to see who was getting out. When a line of kids walked in holding hands, obliged to look at the ground without turning their faces away, many of the mothers started crying. 'Start deciding who's going to be your boyfriend in prison,' said my father. I'm not sure, but I think boys and girls are separated on the inside. He said it to hurt me even more. All my mother did was cry; she didn't say a word.

We were called in to see the judge (I was glad it was a woman). My heart was in my mouth. First my father spoke. Then my mother, who confirmed my rebelliousness and the problems I'd been causing, and said they didn't know what else to do with me and were disappointed. When it was my turn, I lied, saying it was all because I'd been smoking dope. Some of it actually was, but not all of it. I said I regretted what I'd done, although it didn't make any difference to me if I went to prison or home.

When it was the judge's turn, I got the sermon. 'I know your family, I used to work with your sister, and I know they're good people. If I were you, I'd be more grateful. You've gone to good schools, and you have no reason to do what you've done. Since you said the problem is marijuana, I'm not going to do anything with you. I'm going to give you a list of rehab clinics to help you stop. The suit your father has brought against you is going to stay here with me, in a file, because I'm sure this is just a teenage thing that can and will change. I'm not going to put you, who has had an education, in the middle of a group of kids who haven't had (and probably never will have) your opportunities. Since your parents didn't give you a chance, I'm going to give you one, so you can prove you've changed.' And that was it . . .

I didn't end up going to a clinic because my father had sworn never to spend another penny on me, and the clinics were all private and expensive. I actually saw him looking at the list a couple of times, but the subject was never mentioned. His promise to dry up my source of money was strictly kept. I was transferred from São Luís to Brasílio Machado, a state school. They cut my allowance and took me out of the gym. I only received public-transport tickets to go to school. I went from Paraíso to Vila Mariana on foot and sold the tickets for 10 *reais* per week. Almost nothing, but I made do. I was able to buy cigarettes, at least. Go out at night? No way . . . I met a lot of good people at this school, but I also met a lot of bad people, who stole, even though they weren't exactly needy . . . I almost ended up one of them, but I escaped.

There was a Japanese guy who was always after one of the girls at the house on Michigan. But he ended up with me when she turned her nose up at him.

'I've got a fantasy.'

'What?'

'I love shaving pros.'

'But I've hardly got anything –'

'No problem. I want to shave everything off and leave your cunt nice and bare.'

Taking a razor and shaving cream from his bag, my 'Japanese barber' started removing my few pubic hairs. He left me bald. An exciting, new sensation. I tried to initiate sex, but the fantasy session wasn't over. He wanted to take pictures. I let him. It was only after he'd taken loads of pictures that he went down on me. Law of the jungle: you kill it, you eat it. In my case: you peel it, you eat it. Only after this ritual did we actually have sex. In spite of his fetish, we did it in the good, old-fashioned missionary position.

In this profession, we come into contact with a more honest, less hypocritical side of people. They don't hide their most secret desires, and let fetishes out of the bag that they'd never admit to anyone, not even under torture. With a working girl, no one needs to pretend anything. They come to me to indulge their fantasies. We play the role of therapists sometimes. My understanding of normality has changed a lot since I started making a living from sex. Even so, certain situations are hard to forget.

Working in brothels, I have discovered that there are many, many married men, generally between the ages of thirty-five and forty-five, who want you to play the 'active' role.

'Have you got toys?' they ask on the phone.

'Yes, lots.'

'What have you got?'

'Everything. Just tell me what you like to play with.'

'Have you got a vibrator?'

This is a really common question, believe me. Which made me become a regular in sex shops. It's a fun world, as well as perverted. There are lots of 'toys', gels, creams, clothes, costumes, perfumes, lingerie items, and condoms (which I buy to give my clients), as well as a bunch of completely normal-looking people who overcome their shame and go into sex shops in search of excitement. There are enormous dildos, rubber pussies and inflatable dolls on display. It was in one of these sex shops that I saw a guy buying a doll and thought to myself: If one day a boyfriend or husband of mine tells me that he's had sex with one of those things, it'll be the end.

These days I go to a sex shop here in Moema that's such a hoot – only women are allowed in. You feel more at ease, without any guys watching you to see what women buy. And there are some really funny things: a straw and cutlery set in the shape of a penis, which I bought for my place. Sometimes I go just to see what's new. Oops, I almost changed the subject.

Anyway, what these men want is for me to become 'Bruno', stick a huge vibrator in their rear end and really give it to them. I often have to strap on a dildo and give them a good pounding. Modesty aside, I think I do a good job of it. These are guys that you see in the street, family men, your everyday guy. These 'family men' aren't the only ones I've had. I've also fucked lots of pumped-up iron men up the arse – the ones who act all macho and have it in for homosexuals, but who, deep down, between four walls, like to get on all fours and be dominated. I don't think they have the courage to find a guy, and feel less gay if a woman fucks them. At the end of the day, it all becomes 'normal'.

Just as it's normal not to be able to get it up. Only men don't know this . . . One day a tall young man turned up. He was really shy. I hugged him. I'm short, so my ear was pressed against his heart. It was beating fast. As well as shy, he was anxious. We didn't talk much, but I can say it was an 'exotic' encounter. He started sucking my nipples and I noticed something was different. He wasn't sucking – he was suckling! And he stayed there for a while. When he let go, I discreetly pinched my nipples to see if any milk was coming out. Only joking . . .

After the suckling, it was my turn to go down on him. I don't think he'd had a wank for a long time, because his come was very intense and there was a lot of it. His dick throbbed in my mouth for ages. I went to the bathroom to get cleaned up and when I came back he took my hand and placed it on his limp dick. Wow! He didn't even want to take a quick break! I went back to sucking his limp dick. I stayed at it for half an hour. There's nothing worse than sucking a limp dick. And no sign of it coming back to life. He's lucky I didn't charge for the millilitres of saliva I spent that day. He got angry and swore at his dick, complaining as if he were talking to it. He was embarrassed at not being able to get it up for the second round. I'm not surprised – I've never seen someone go two rounds without a breather. He ended up going into the bathroom for a wank to see if he could get it up again. How did I know? I could see his shadow on the door. A typical case of a problem with the upstairs head.

A period with two different sentences. This was what came of the fight with my father. I needed to escape and go and live my life before he decided how I should live it. In that house of locked doors I was a kind of human guinea pig. First the locked doors, then the recordings, and now total silence. No one spoke to me any more. I only had my cat to keep me company. Me, who hates being alone.

One night I overheard my parents talking about sending me away, although they didn't say where. I didn't even know what to think. I felt like a little girl again, alone, still and petrified in a dark room, scared as I had always been (and still am), imagining a monster under my bed. In my case, it slept in the bedroom next door – and its evil seemed to be an unconfessable secret. If I'd escaped being sent to the juvenile detention centre, what could he have in mind? It was the darkest and longest night of my life.

One day in July, out of the blue, my mother told me I was going to Guarujá the next day. Now who, after a crazy story like this, sends their daughter off to have fun on the beach? I realised, in part due to her silence, that this wasn't a sign of regret. They really were planning something for me and wanted me out of there.

Can you believe that my father only gave me 50 *reais* to last two weeks? OK, so I was going to stay at a friend's place, but that wouldn't even last a day. And it didn't. Since I didn't want to take anyone else's money, not even if they lent it to me, it occurred to me to have sex for money. I don't even know where I got this idea, but off I went. I went out alone one night to walk along the pavement and flirt with men who were alone. If someone came on to me, I'd tell them I was a prostitute and that they'd have to pay if they wanted to have sex with me. Several men stopped and some even came close. But I didn't have the courage to say a thing. It wasn't something I wanted or knew how to do. I didn't know how to sell my body. I gave up and borrowed some money from a friend who was keen on me. He gave me 150 *reais*. 'Pay me back when you can.' I never saw him again . . .

I returned from this trip truly happy, which I hadn't felt for a long time, and I don't know why but my parents didn't even look away from the TV when I sang out, 'I'm home!' My mother never spoke to me again. I couldn't have cared less if my father never looked me in the face again. But never again to hear my mother call me 'daughter' in that comforting voice of hers was perhaps the closest I'd ever been to the solitude of death. I never wanted to feel like that again. Never again.

* * *

The uncomfortable silence dragged through the days, heavy. Whatever it was they'd thought about doing with me, like sending me to a boarding school, emancipating me so they could kick me out of home, or something like that, I wasn't sticking around to find out. My time was running out. I started buying newspapers for the classifieds. I realised that my inexperience was going to be an insurmountable obstacle. All paths led to the only thing a girl like me could do. That was how I began my pilgrimage through the houses that placed ads in newspapers for girls between the ages of eighteen and twenty-five looking to earn '1000 *reais* per week'.

I visited massage parlours, brothels and even nightclubs. On 8 October 2002, twenty days before my eighteenth birthday, I summoned the courage to tell my father that I was going to leave home and get a job. Repeating that he wasn't going to give me another penny if I left, he asked how I intended to survive. In my incredible naivety, although determined to confront him, I said I was going to be a masseuse for executives. But I really believed it, because that's what the ads said: massage. A girl in one house I visited had said that just a massage was one price, and if the client wanted sex, he'd pay the difference. I was going to just stick to the massage. Of course, he flew into a rage. I was ready and willing for him to beat me again.

But instead of a heavy hand came a voice, confused, disorientated, disconcerted. He started talking to me. Upset, yes. Angry, yes. But he did try to talk to me. But it was too late to start talking. He really didn't have the slightest vocation for it. And I went on, sincerely, in my naivety, 'But, Dad, it's just massage, not sex. I'm not going to have sex, I'm just going to give massages.' Everything he hadn't said in my life, and especially since the 'law of silence' had been laid down in our house, he vomited up that night. What he really wanted was to convince me not to leave. I listened in silence. My silence got him even more worked up. You little whore . . . slut . . . His words came out in an endless string, as if he didn't even need to stop to breathe.

He was worn out and the conversation ended when almost a death-sentence (or perhaps wish) escaped his lips. 'All prostitutes get Aids. I'm really sorry that you're going die alone of Aids at Emílio Ribas Hospital.' Fine. If being free meant I had to be a prostitute, then that's what I was going to be. And if that meant I had to die, then so be it.

I'd already had sex with lots of men. Some I couldn't even remember. Of course there were others who were unforgettable. Like a really insecure guy that showed up one day. He clearly had problems. He was sad. Like someone who is far away, talking to himself, he started singing along with the music that was playing. The scene moved me, I must confess. Here was a man who needed refuge. But that wasn't why he'd booked me. When I saw his naked body, I got a shock. First, because the guy was really skinny. Second, his dick was huge! I think it was the biggest I'd ever seen. The sex was awful, because I was worried about what he was feeling. He needed help and I didn't know what to do . . . I also had a hard time sucking him off. He was so big that only his little head (so to speak) fitted in my mouth. Getting a condom on him was a nightmare. It was too tight and made him lose his hard-on. Even so, we managed to have a bit of sex. It was one of the few times I felt a guy's dick hit my uterus. A new sensation, anyway. He came while wanking off over my tits, emptied out a litre of come and went. I was left with the odd impression that something had been missing in that session. What? Perhaps I should have said something. Or maybe it was just my impression. But I knew very well what it was like to feel unhappy . . .

By December 2003, I'd already bought myself a computer. It was a way to fill my moments of solitude. I'd always loved surfing the Internet and had discovered blogs. Everyone had their own and it looked interesting, fun. I decided to run a Google search for blogs by working girls, just to see what their lives were like, the day-to-day life of another girl like myself, to compare. You can find everything on the Internet, can't you? Well surprise surprise – no hits! I searched again, using every available search engine. Nothing!

I was alone a lot, which I hate. It scares me, I don't know why. I'd met a girl who was really nice – Gabi, who rented a flat in the same building as me and who is now my best friend. One night when I was feeling down, I called her over the intercom and asked her to come and keep me company, but she couldn't. I almost went crazy. So I decided to write in my blog everything I'd wanted to tell her that night. Someone would see it. Who knows, maybe even my family would see it. What I really wanted was for someone to come to my aid, save me. From my life, my story. From me.

I was really down. I wrote a sketch of my life and said that prostitution wasn't worth it and that if I could turn back the clock I'd never have chosen this path. All this in a working girl's blog . . . The next day I was feeling a little better and decided to delete everything. People were going to think that, as well as a pro, I was crazy. I think all this happened because Christmas was near. I thought about my mother, home. My enthusiasm for the blog cooled somewhat and I forgot about it for a while.

On 1 January 2004, I thought: I'm going to go back to my blog. Since it was a kind of diary, it made sense to start that day. I decided to write about my daily life instead of just offloading. And I'd also be able to record in a different way everything that I wrote in my agenda, especially details about each client. I'd always thought about doing a more in-depth statistical study when I left prostitution. For example, I'm 100 per cent certain that 70 per cent of my clients are married. I always ask them why they're cheating on their wives, not to mention paying for sex. There are only two kinds of answer. They're tired of having sex with their wives or afraid to tell their wives their fantasies because they're too prudish. Only 20 per cent are diehard bachelors who don't have time or can't be bothered going out (or can't pick anyone up), and the other 10 per cent are engaged or committed.

I never imagined that other people would find it all so interesting. But I thought it would be fun for me. Imagine being able to classify sex, say what it was like. This was how I came up with my 'categories':

– Mechanical: there's no chemistry, when I'm tired and impatient. I keep glancing at the clock and watching the time, which doesn't pass. I do everything begrudgingly, although I do everything I can to make the client come quickly and leave. Sometimes I even sigh loudly. 'Shall we change position?' the client asks. Completely bored, I answer, 'Humph', since I can't swear. . . . I don't even go to the trouble of moaning.

– Couple: there's chemistry, as if we were a real couple having sex for the first time, at a motel, kissing, hugging, caresses, careful sex, the missionary position.

– Smutty: does smutty need explaining? I feel like a real prostitute, and I let it all hang out. I don't really know how to explain it . . . With couple sex, even when it's hot, I don't feel like a prostitute. In this case I do.

My blog was hosted in the Terra website. One night, when I went to make a post, I typed in my password and a message appeared saying it was wrong. It was a Friday and I'd have to wait until the following Monday to resolve the problem.

On the Sunday, I decided to try again and, to my surprise, I saw there was a new post and, worse, it wasn't what I had written! I realised that someone must have hacked my computer and stolen my password . . . I was so angry I cried!

On the Monday, I called Terra and managed to

get in touch with the person responsible for the blogs. I explained what had happened and they managed to restore my password after a week. The person continued posting every day, pretending to be me.

I got scared that this person might write something compromising. But it didn't happen. The person was happy just imitating me, and they did it so well that I actually thought I'd written some of those posts.

I got my password back, deleted everything I hadn't written and explained what had happened to my readers. A month had barely gone by when my password was stolen again. This time it was much worse, because not only did the person pretend to be me, but they also posted Word files stolen from my computer. They were very compromising, since some chapters of my book were copied and pasted into the blog.

This time I cried even more and lost several nights' sleep, wondering who might have done it and why. I managed to recover my password again, but I gave up on the blog. Until a friend who works with computers suggested I get my own site, where I could continue my blog and also post my photos.

It was with this site that I started to taste success. The photos helped me gain the trust of people who didn't believe that the blog was written by a real working girl. I'd received lots of emails from people who didn't believe me. Many of them thought I was a man dreaming it all up.

It was with this change of address that my blog started making waves. Many people thought – and still think – that my stolen passwords were just a marketing ploy to get attention.

My blog suddenly had so many visitors that I got a fright. Something so startling was going on that the guys at iBest, the host site, called to tell me my blog was the second most visited link. I had no idea it would go so far. At first, I was frightened. It's strange thinking that lots of people know what's going on in your life. It was as if they'd invaded my house and rummaged through my drawers. At the same time, I discovered that that was exactly what I wanted – for people to read about my life. At least my public life. Not Raquel's, but Bruna's.

I went to bed for the last time in that flat. Our talk had really upset me. My father didn't trust me at all. Not even in my ability to look after myself. He made me feel useless. I promised myself it was the last time I'd allow that to happen. With him or any other man on the face of this earth. I oscillated between moments of distress and great excitement. In a few hours, I'd be free to go wherever I wanted, to do whatever I wanted.

A WORKING GIRL'S
DIARY

Wednesday, 28 June

FIRST CLIENT

Client profile: a bit nutty at first. Later, he was OK. And really naughty. There was no chemistry or affinity.

Classification: mechanical.

Interesting fact: he slipped his dick into my cunt thinking it was my arse. But it wasn't my fault. I swear.

Funny fact: he swore I'd smoked pot. It wasn't true. I swear.

Round one: we went down on each other, but neither of us came. Just as well. Then I rode him until his eyes rolled back in his head.

Round two: I got on all fours and we had anal . . . oops . . . vaginal sex until he came.

Since June 2004, my posts in www.brunasurfistinha.com have all been like this. Standardised, very simple, without many details. I had up to ten clients a day. I didn't have much time to write, just enough between clients to jot things down on a piece of paper to type up later on the computer. Even so, due to the blog, I inspired the fantasies of many boys and men as they wanked themselves off. And I gained a certain fame. It wasn't exactly what I'd been seeking, but since it had happened . . .

In August 2004, the magazine *Época* interviewed me and a special edition of the magazine *Capricho* did a story on me. I gave an interview to *Vip*, several newspapers and a couple of porno magazines. I appeared in a number of websites, participated in online chats and, one day I was invited to appear on the TV programme *Superpop*, hosted by Luciana Gimenez. It was a double opportunity.

Firstly, I'd be able to show my face so people would believe I actually existed and was really me. Yes, lots of false Brunas were beginning to pop up all over the place using my name, like a certain Samara, who passed herself off as me in the online community *Orkut* and even created a community: ENOUGH OF BRUNA, THE SURFER GIRL.

Secondly, I believed my parents would see me and realise that, although I'm in prostitution, I'm fine. I'm not rotting in a corner. That's what I was thinking when I gave the interviews. I even went on the radio station Jovem Pan's programme *Pânico* (lots of fun). By the way, they were really nice. I was worried they were going to have a laugh at my expense – but they didn't. They even avoided inviting listeners to ask questions. I guess there's a lesson in it for all of us. I hope that one day, when this is all over, I can have a relationship with my parents again.

The day I went on *Superpop*, the exposure started to make itself felt before I'd even gone on air – or left home. The production car arrived at my building and the driver asked the doorman to let me know they'd arrived. The doorman, of course, asked if I was going to be on TV and, obviously, watched the programme, which is live. Needless to say, word got around. It didn't change the way the employees here treat me. There was just one time that the building manager got on my case, saying that the other residents were complaining that I brought a lot of men here. I'd never seen a soul in the corridor . . . He was the one who had a problem with it. When they saw that I'd become 'famous', however, it stopped. They started treating me with even more respect (not that anyone had ever treated me badly).

Thursday, 13 July

I'd always wondered what it would be like to have sex with a call boy. Were they as diligent as I was with my clients? Were they able to please a woman, get her nice and wet and make her come for real? There were lots of call boys living in the same building as me. All really cute, but trying hard to cultivate a bad-boy image or a swish, designer look. Since curiosity always speaks loudest, especially to me, I decided to give one a try. I can't even begin to describe it. It was . . . it was . . . HORRIBLE! We were like two little sex-machines: him faking it on the one hand while I faked it on the other. It was like choreography: I trotted out my tricks and he did his. Kiss, suck, lick, stick it in. Really strange. But that wasn't the worst of it. I was completely turned off when I remembered that most of his clients were men. Modesty aside, I think I manage to be a little bit less mechanical with my clients. And, since I wasn't paying (neither was he), there was no reason for it to be a 'free sample' of professional sex . . .

I realised that my blog, as well as attracting a lot of people who didn't used to be my clients, could also be 'something extra' for my clients to enjoy. They love seeing my assessment of their performance. So much so that I have a notice: THE 'MOST INTER-ESTING' OR 'BEST' PERFORMANCES OF THE WEEK. IF YOU'VE VISITED ME IN THIS PER-IOD AND I'VE FAILED TO MENTION YOU, DON'T WORRY. TRY AGAIN WHEN YOU CAN . . . And a lot of them really do try several times. Good for business, isn't it?

When things stabilised at an average of five or six clients a day (from Monday to Friday, only after lunch), I decided to spice up my blog. But always taking care not to reveal the identity of my clients. Only they know who I'm talking about. There are things like tattoos, or the location of a piercing, or some detail of their body or personality that can give them away. Which is not my intention. There are prostitutes who end up making their clients' lives hell, blackmailing them even. But this is defi-nitely not my cup of tea. I get my kicks from other things.

Something everyone always asks is if I actually feel pleasure with my clients. The answer is yes. No matter how professional it is, if there's chemistry, affinity and the guy turns me on, why shouldn't I make the most of it? After all, playing is my job. I'm paid to indulge other people's fantasies. (I have my own, but I keep them to myself. As a 'business woman', I have my professional routine and a 'Bruna quality standard' to keep up).

In spite of this playful side to my work and getting to meet a lot of people, I confess that I sometimes feel lonely. I don't like being on my own. I need to care for someone and feel that someone cares for me. I'm not a machine. I sense something good's going to happen when the client really wants to give me pleasure. If that's what he wants, why not give it to him? Or at least try. Of course, sometimes it just doesn't happen. Not even with what I like to call 'inner effort' – Kegal exercises using the pelvic-floor muscles, which potentialise the strength of an orgasm. I use this technique with the clients who really want me to come. To come more quickly . . . These certainly don't go in my blog . . .

In spite of the life I lead, I've managed to have a few boyfriends, as well as a lot of flings. The last one lasted four months. I know, not long. But, for someone with a life like mine, it was a long time. We met through a mutual friend. Well, he wasn't a friend, until he became one. This guy called me several times, and we started chatting a lot. With me, when you're a friend, there's no sex. I don't have sex with my friends. One night, I was hanging out at my place with Gabi and I told him to come over and bring a friend for her.

No fooling around. I was looking for company, to shoot the breeze, and if something happened it would be personal. He did bring a friend – my boyfriend! When we saw each other, it was like something out of a film, devastating and mutual. He knew who I was, what I did and everything. Even so, I went with him that night and we started seeing each other. It felt great. Once again I was just a girl who liked a guy and felt something for him.

Our relationship was like that of any girl my age. We went out, watched films, went dancing, hung out at home, laughed, talked and, of course, had sex. I know how to separate the sex of my work from sex with my boyfriend – with love, lust, or whatever it is that drives the relationship. My head and body might be tired, but when I'm with my partner I want to have real sex. Sometimes, I have to make an effort. But it's awful not to give attention to the person you're with. After all, the guy already has to deal with the fact that his girlfriend is a pro. How could I let him go without sex? Even though he knew all about me from the outset, like the others before him, after a while he found he couldn't handle the fact of my profession and all the hype about the blog, my 'fifteen minutes of fame'. What a shame. These minutes will pass and I'll still be here, being myself.

Amidst all the razzle-dazzle, all the attention I was getting because of the interviews and, of course, the TV shows, there were people who already knew me and called me up just to talk. On the other hand, there were also people who called to remind me that being a pro has its price in any day and age. A kid who had gone to school with me at Bandeirantes called and really got me down. 'Well, Raquel, who would have imagined? A pro!' What hurt most is that he wanted to hurt me. 'Everyone that studied with us is in their second or third year of university and you're the only one that's a pro.' He put me down, and got to me in a way I didn't want him to. Of course I'd already thought about these things, and the lives of the people who'd gone to school with me: they were all progressing. To this day I'm not really sure why he did that. He didn't gain anything, insulting me like that. Still, what did I expect?

There are those who think that prostitutes don't have needs. How silly. It's like saying that cooks don't get hungry. That must be why, although sex was my work, I was always masturbating. I wanted to enjoy my own fantasies. The last time I went with someone as a 'civilian', the guy ended up getting fired. That's right! The person who told me the outcome of the story was Natália, a friend who swells the numbers in group sex when the clients don't bring other girls. We'd gone to a normal nightclub, just for fun, in Jardins. I mentioned it in my blog, saying what club it had been at (some grass probably read it and the guy got fired as a result). I felt bad, but he was the one who was working, not me . . . I'd drunk a lot. When that happens I'm really easy, I lose control. Actually, in my opinion, all women become easy and turned on in this situation.

The club is divided into two parts. I was upstairs, where he was working as a waiter at the bar. I noticed him staring at me – and I stared back, of course, openly flirting. When I went to get another beer at the counter, he flirted back and I couldn't help myself – I kissed him. I asked for a paper napkin to write my number on so we could meet elsewhere. 'No, I've got an idea. I'll go into the bathroom, you wait a minute, then follow me in. We can have a quickie in there.' It was more than half an hour . . . When we came out, there was a huge queue at the door. The bathroom is unisex and I was so embarrassed as I walked out. It had been ages since I'd had sex with whoever I wanted. I needed to have sex like that, with someone I was interested in – and not for money.

I'd already given up hope of ever being involved with someone. But, on Valentine's Day, 2005, I felt like a normal girl again – someone asked me to be his girlfriend. That's right!!! It was Pedro. He was married and was always saying his marriage was on the rocks, but he hadn't separated because of his two young daughters. He'd never been with a prostitute, but he followed my blog, was curious to meet me, and, as he said, became my fan. He ended up visiting me seven times, from the time we met until we became friends. He'd separated from his wife a few months before.

On Valentine's Day, surprise surprise! He asked me to go out with him. He'd already insinuated that he'd support me financially if I wanted to give up prostitution. I explained (and he was mature enough to understand) that I'd left my parents' home to be independent. He respects me and handles being with me just fine. So much so that we now live together and have plans for the future. I think he's the love of my life. My mother would certainly love him. I always joke with him, saying that experience has taught me all the excuses husbands tell their wives when they're cheating on them. He'll have to be really creative if he ever feels tempted . . . Poor Pedro.

Thursday, 7 August

FIFTH CLIENT

Yay! Finally someone invited me to a swingers' club!!! We arrived at 11 p.m. and left at 4 a.m. He'd already gone out with me three times before. I was left with a weird feeling at the end of the evening. I ended up crying in the couples' room. It was packed, but it wasn't nice, even though there were lots of beautiful people there. There were lots of young guys on their own, lots of hard-to-please women and, in the maze, on Thursdays, unaccompanied men are allowed in. In other words, you can't go in there, because they're like vultures to a carcass. It's true. But the music was excellent, with lots of old classics. They even played one of my favourites (I don't know the name, but I know it's by The Mamas & The Papas).

Unfortunately for the men, Thursday is also the day when there is a strip show just for the ladies. I wasn't pulled into the middle of the show, as usually happens. Partly because I didn't feel like it. We switched couples three times, but only one of the women was worth it for me. With the first couple, the girl was really sexy, but she didn't go with women, unfortunately for me. When I took my top off, she squeezed my breast and said, 'It's silicone, isn't it, hon?' Calling me 'hon', especially during sex, was a turn-off. I laughed in her face. I don't like it when people call me 'honey'. Much less 'hon'.

Her partner was also an annoying young guy who wanted to come on my tits. I refused, but he insisted. I don't like it when someone insists on something I don't feel like doing, so I ended up saying it was OK. Just when he was about to come, I got back at him – I moved away and not a drop of come fell on me. The second swap was with a Japanese guy who I actually quite liked, but when we got down to business, I didn't enjoy it. We were having sex with me on all fours on the sofa and him standing. He was really pounding me. I turned my face to one side to avoid slamming my nose straight into the wall. I ended up banging my head anyway. I saw stars. He was a bit aggressive, but luckily he came quickly. My client pretended to come with the 'hon' so they'd leave quickly and we could have sex by ourselves. With me, he came.

After the third swap (I didn't have the courage to touch the girl, although I was dying to go down on her), a really drunk guy grabbed me and said that the minute he'd seen me he'd remembered the film *Scent of a Woman*, and started telling me the plot.

For God's sake, no one needs to hear the synopsis of a film in the middle of a swingers' club.

Before the third swap, we stopped in the maze. A woman of about forty and her husband were busy groping each other, but she was sucking off another guy. She was a confirmed dick-sucker. Out of the blue, another dick appeared and she shoved it in her mouth. Suddenly, all kinds of men started appearing from all over the place to be sucked off by the woman. By my count, she sucked seven dicks. At one stage I thought they were going to start taking a number and joining the queue. Oh well, whatever. Though come to think of it, even I – a pro – would never suck seven dicks at a swingers' club.

I noticed she didn't look up. She didn't even know who all those dicks belonged to. She just grabbed them and shoved them in her mouth. All I could think about was the sort of guys they were – not exactly the best catch, to be really polite. Who am I to criticise anyone? But I have to admit, I was shocked. It was probably her fantasy. I'm not sure if I was more disgusted by the woman or the men. Men are UN-FREAKING-BELIEVABLE! When they get turned on, they stick their dicks in the first hole they see. They only don't stick them in a hole in the wall because holes in walls don't moan.

I still hadn't gone down on a woman. We were in the room where only couples can enter and one started touching me. Then she suggested that we go into a private room. We went down on each other for ages. I didn't manage to come, but she came in my mouth. Her pussy was the way I like them, nice and fleshy.

From all the relationships I've had while working in this profession, I've learnt that men will only respect me as a woman again the day I give it up. And another thing I've learnt – when this happens and I meet the man of my dreams, the one I'm going to marry and have kids with, I'm not going to tell him that I used to be a working girl. I've decided I want to leave it all in the past. Forget? No, that's impossible . . . Let's just say that I'm going to put all this life experience in a drawer and never open it again. I'll no doubt be scared he might already have met me as Bruna or find out some other way. But I must make it clear – I don't regret what I've done. I hope with Pedro things will be different, because I love him very much and hope he is able to respect me.

One of the classic Cinderella dreams of working girls is finding the man who will take them out of prostitution. Would you believe it happened to me? It was a sixty-two-year-old client, who was a widower and very lonely. He came to me each week, but we almost never had sex; we mostly just talked (this is more common than you would imagine). One day he came right out and said, 'I want to have a serious talk with you.' He told me that his son, who lived with him, was going on exchange for a year, and he was going to be alone. He invited me to live with him and asked me to give up prostitution. He'd pay for whatever I wanted: studies, gym, clothes, spending-money, as long as I gave it all up.

I said I'd think about it and I really did. In reality, I wouldn't be giving up prostitution, but I'd only be doing it with him, also for money. A single client for the rest of his life (which could be quite a while). My refusal had nothing to do with him, since I got along well with him, nor his generous offer, because no one was fooling anyone there. But I'd left my parents' home to have more freedom. To tie myself to a man, unless it was for love, would be like swapping one cage for another. A gold one, yes, but a cage nonetheless. I know it would have been a good deal for me, and that I was turning down the offer of a lifetime for many girls like me, but I was also afraid that he might die and I'd be blamed for it. I think I've seen this kind of thing in too many films, as well as real life.

It's not every day that someone decides to 'save your soul by watching over your body', but after being with the same client many times, it often turns into a friendship. These days, all of my friends are former clients. My best friend came to me five or six times as a client. And on several occasions the sex took a back seat. We started to touch base daily, not just to schedule a fuck. One day, I had to make things very clear: 'The minute we become friends, there's no more sex.' I can't, it doesn't work. I don't like having sex with my friends. If you're a friend, the professional relationship is over.

Tuesday, 12 September

THIRD CLIENT

I went to a little party with three guys, and a girl, but one of the guys only wanted to watch. We arranged to meet at the All Black bar and from there we went to one of their flats. It was a quiet little group session. First, I went with one in the bedroom. We had a bit of sex but he only came afterwards, in my mouth. Then we hung around drinking and chatting with the other two in the living room, while the girl went into the bedroom with the one I'd been with. I ended up lying on the sofa while one guy went down on me. To make life easier, I helped him with my finger and had an amazing orgasm. The other one just sat on the other sofa watching us. When the other two left the bedroom, the two of us went in. I rode him for a while, then he came in my mouth.

Interesting fact: one of them had been my client before.

Sad fact: I got home at five-thirty in the morning . . .

The gynaecologist plays an important role in a working girl's everyday life. And he has to know what I do. There's no two ways about it. How else can he give me the right advice, examine me as carefully as I need him to in order to protect me? AIDS is the biggest fear. I get tested every three months and it's always the same agony. I'm always afraid when I go. Yes, I protect myself, I always use condoms . . . That is, there is no way the snake's going in unprotected during sex. But I admit I take a chance in oral sex.

The doctor told me the chances of catching something are smaller in oral sex, but they're there. Especially if I have a small sore in my mouth, which is the kind of thing you often don't even know you have. I don't know . . . Sometimes I think the client looks safe, I feel comfortable, trust what I'm seeing and go down on him 'à la natural'. The regret comes later. You can't tell if a guy has something just by looking at him. But I never swallow. I even let the guy come in my mouth, and I like it, but I never swallow (well, not very often). I'd say that five out of ten times I'm silly enough to give blow jobs without condoms. But I want to do this less and less.

Looking after one's body without looking after one's head would be silly, wouldn't it? Health OK, hair OK (much to the envy of lots of women, my hair is really straight, and I don't need to use a flat iron – lucky, aren't I?), moisturised skin, finger-nails always well-kept.

When this is all in order, I take some time for myself. Every Monday afternoon I have therapy. It's funny, because I've been to psychologists all my life. It's different now, though.

In the beginning, I didn't know who I was taking to the sessions: Raquel or Bruna. These days it's not so difficult. I've been through the phase of wanting to tell my therapist my whole life story, which is the most difficult and complicated part. Now, I always sum up the week, how things affect Raquel, my outlook on life, my plans. And obviously, amidst so much talk about me, I also end up mentioning some clients and the things we did. You can't just shut them out.

Friday, 22 September

FOURTH CLIENT

Appearances can be deceptive . . . Once, over in the house on Alameda Franca, a really good-looking guy picked me. I liked the look of him. He had a naughty air about him but he also seemed like a nice guy. And he looked like he'd be good in bed. While we chatted intimately in the waiting room, deciding what was going to happen, he made a request: he wanted me to fuck him in the arse. OK, no problem. He wouldn't be the first or last guy I'd do as 'Bruno'. He wanted me to come into the room already wearing the strap-on. The client's wish is my command, right? But when it was time to get it from behind, he started playing hard-to-get, trying to get away from me, jumping forward. He'd fantasised about being fucked, but didn't have the courage. As soon as the dildo touched his arse he'd try to get away. But he spent ages greedily sucking the rubber dick. We had three sessions like this.

The fourth time he showed up, he asked if I had a male friend who could come in for a threesome and, of course, give it to him in the arse. So was that it?

The guy actually wanted a real dick, but had come to a pro so he wouldn't feel queer. I joked that the security guard might be able to do him a favour, but he took me seriously. He asked how much he'd charge to have sex with us. Of course he wasn't going to accept, but I had to pretend. I went down-stairs and told the other girls the whole story and they fell about laughing. Then I went back upstairs and told him the security guard had turned down the offer. He was really disappointed and looked like a lost puppy. I didn't end up doing him in the arse. I wonder if he's still a virgin or if he's finally worked up the courage to let someone pop his cherry.

There are people who are scared to call me be-cause of the price. Sure, there are girls who charge 300, 400 *reais*, but they only have one, two, or three clients a week at the most. I know that with my 'fame' as Bruna, the Surfer Girl, I could even charge more. But I like what I do, I won't deny it. It makes me feel wanted, something I never used to be. And, obviously, there's the practical side. I'm a practical person: the more clients I have, the more money I make. I don't waste time negotiat-ing prices. Lots of guys try to haggle for discounts, advantages, exclusivity. I can't be bothered with any of it.

Friday 10 November

FIFTH CLIENT

Getting asked to a swingers' club is a prize that all call girls love. I went to a really up-market club in Moema with an amazing client – he never got tired of fucking me and all the other women we went with while we were there. That was when he wasn't wildly wanking off as he watched me with the women he was going to fuck or had already fucked. And he came every single time. I saw it with my own eyes!

Now there's a place at this club that I love. It's this tiny room, just the right size for a couple. Those on the outside can peer through a glass window at about eye-level, but it's almost impossible to see what's going on inside, because the glass is for the people on the inside to see who's outside. Get the picture? It's a turn-on for those who like to be seen but deep down only want to have the 'sensation' of being seen. But this is just a starter – and those outside aren't left twiddling their thumbs. There are two holes in the wall between the room and the corridor, right underneath this window. You can stick your hands through and touch the people getting it on in the room. My client and I were instantly addicted: we spent two hours groping everything that came near the hole: arses, tits, dicks . . . That was when a couple invited us in with them. What a crazy feeling! We saw the hungry eyes of those who couldn't see us, while we felt hands blindly groping for any bit of skin within reach. It's a huge turn-on. And with a big advantage: we only let the people we found attractive touch us – the lookers and the sexy ones.

It's a shame it took me so long to discover this place. I didn't come at all because there wasn't enough space to lie down, and I can't have an orgasm standing up, but I had a great time anyway. It didn't detract from the night at all. And I solved the problem with my magic finger: I went home and masturbated. After I'd come, tired and happy, I closed my eyes and dreamed sweet dreams.

The same way I entered this life, I know I'm going to leave. I don't want to be a pro for the rest of my life. That's what I work towards. First, I got rid of the pimps. No way am I giving half or more of what I earn to someone. Yes, there's a down side to working alone, which is the lack of security. Receiving clients in a serviced flat helps a little. And I always get their phone number – and confirm that it's really theirs. 'What's your phone number? That way, if something comes up, I can call and cancel. Since they always make appointments a few hours in advance, it's cool. To this day, I've never had problems with aggressive clients. Just as well, isn't it? Truth be told, my biggest fear is running across one of my father's or sisters' friends. I've already had people I knew as clients, including former classmates from Bandeirantes (who didn't recognise me, but I made a point of saying, 'I remember you from somewhere, but not here – we went to school together').

Wednesday, 22 November

SECOND CLIENT

Whatever turns people on is fine by me but sometimes you can't help wondering . . . A client arrived at my flat and took off all his clothes, but left his socks on. The sex was mechanical for me, because I couldn't concentrate. I wanted to know why he hadn't taken his socks off. Did he have really ugly feet? Or maybe he had sores or something. He seemed really relaxed, had a good shag and came twice, once with me sucking his dick and once with me riding him. I led the session, because I didn't want to see his feet in socks. They were ordinary men's socks, no holes, nothing special. He went to have a shower after he'd come for the second time and I sat in the bedroom, perplexed. Suddenly, I heard, 'WHAT THE FUCK?' almost shouted from the bathroom and I ran to see what had happened. There he was, starkers, showering . . . with his socks on! Would you believe he'd simply forgotten to take them off both to have sex and to shower? We had a good laugh. Men!

By myself, working Monday to Friday, I have twenty-five to thirty clients a week. There are days when I have more than five, but more than that gets a bit much. Each session here in my flat lasts an hour and, for 200 *reais*, they can have oral and vaginal sex. If they want anal sex, it's 250 *reais* (after my appearance on *Pânico*, in June, I decided to put my prices up a little due to the higher demand. Before that, for a reeaaaally long time, I charged 150 and 200, respectively). As many times as they want in an hour. And they don't have to pay for a motel, flat, anything. It's all included. Unless the client wants to go to a motel or have me visit him in a hotel room (then I charge double, because of the travel time). With this system, I give myself the weekends off. That's how it is for everyone else, isn't it? Why should it be different for a working girl?

Even seeing what I do in business terms, I admit I've felt sorry for clients before. I remember thinking: This guy saved up for ages to be here with me. How did I know? It was all in 1-*real* notes. No kidding! I think it was change from his bus money, this and that. He scraped together 150 *reais* in 1-*real* notes. He looked really embarrassed.

'Do you mind if I pay you like this?'

'No, that's fine.'

He handed me that bunch of notes and I counted it while he finished getting dressed. At the time, I felt a twinge of pity. Imagine what it took to save it all. But fuck for free, no way. Pity is one thing but business is business.

Another thing I've realised in this profession is that it has its peaks and troughs. I already mentioned that demand increases at the start of winter. It also happens at the end of the year, when people receive their Christmas bonuses. They can't afford it normally. So some guys make the most of the extra money. It gives you a certain pride to know that the guy worked the whole year and gave himself a fuck with you for Christmas. Which is probably why these are the ones who make the most of it.

An interesting side of freelancing is acting according to your own rules and convictions. Creating your own service standard. Remember the story about the towels and bed linen? Well, for clients, and for me, hygiene is basic. So here at my place, there's a towel for each client. I sometimes joke that when I leave the profession, I won't know what to do with them. On a few occasions, I let the laundry pile get out of control and, by the time I realised, there weren't many clean ones. I had to buy new ones. I've got a collection – almost eighty! They're all white, because then you can see that they really are clean. My clients' soap is liquid (I hate those revolting bars of soap full of hairs, *arghh*, passing from client to client). Unless a client sweats a lot or gets gel on the sheets, I make them last at least two sessions, without any problems. I supply the condoms. Unless the client is extra-large, in which case they generally bring their own in the right size.

Monday, 4 December

FIRST CLIENT

We repeated the party. The same guys as last time. But today there were only two, the voyeur and the owner of the flat. Unfortunately, the cowboy wasn't there . . . Like the other times, the party went smoothly. As well as myself, there was also the other girl. While I got with the voyeur in the living room, the other two went into the bedroom. In the beginning, I felt weird, because the voyeur (who did NOT just look this time) had never been with a pro. And what's more: he'd never cheated before!!! An almost perfect man, right? At least until today . . . He asked me if not cheating was good or bad. Don't ask what my answer was. He was really affectionate with me . . . The foreplay lasted ages, then I gave him a blow job and he came really fast. Then we waited to do the 'swap'. The other guy came out of the bedroom and jumped on me with a hard-on. He went down on me, then went for it in the missionary position until he came.

I got a huge fright. One night, I had a really bad craving and started snorting. I have no idea how much coke I did. At one stage it felt like I was no longer inside myself. My body refused to respond. My breathing was strange. There was a weird taste in my mouth. Overdose. I looked in the mirror and saw myself dead: drained of colour, dry mouth, purple lips. My heart was beating so fast it felt like it was going to explode. I blacked out. I'm a Spiritualist, because I believe that on the 'other side' there is everything that we have here. Even hospitals. When I came to, I could swear I was in a hospital 'on the other side.' It was a bad trip. Everything felt unreal (to this day I don't know if I imagined, saw, or dreamed it all), but I remember talking a lot with a man, I don't know who, who told me a bunch of things. Including that I had to stop snorting. When I really came to I realised there were no men there. From this day on I promised myself I was going to stop.

Once clean, I was steadfast in my decision. It was difficult, of course. I had bouts of cold turkey and thought I was dying every time it happened. Gabi helped me a lot during this period, giving me support and putting up with me in that state. I kind of went into self-imposed seclusion at home. I stopped going out at night, because I knew where to find coke easily and didn't want to do it any more. Whenever I felt a craving, that crazy urge to snort coming on, I thought about my life, that dream (imagination or hallucination), of the man in the hospital. I remembered that I'd gone into this profession with the intention of stopping. But at one stage I was spending as much as 50, 70 *reais* a day snorting 4 grams of coke. The purest, the most expensive. No chalk or marble dust. It was more than 50 per cent of what I earned. I'd get nowhere at this rate. Or perhaps only to the hospital on the 'other side.'

After I decided to give up coke, I stayed a little more on track with my objectives and saw what a fool I'd been. That's why everything that comes easily goes even more easily . . . 'Easy' money is also addictive. And I don't want to spend the rest of my life in prostitution. This, together with the fact that I'm very practical, inspired me to come up with a plan to help me stay on track. I call it my '500 nest-egg goal'. Lots of people think it means saving 500,000 *reais*. But that's not exactly it.

In the beginning, when I left home, I thought I was going to be in prostitution for the rest of my life. With time, I saw that it's taxing work, both physically and psychologically. In 2004 it occurred to me to give it all up and go back to school. Truth be told, the penny dropped that I had to give it up. I don't know when, but I have to stop one day. But in order to do so, I had to have an objective, a goal. So one day I sat down and dreamed big, thinking about how much a flat would cost. I did several calculations of things I wanted to buy, and how much I'd need to buy them and leave this life behind, taking into consideration what I'd already saved. The result was ridiculous, something like 500 grand. I'd need a lot of clients to make that kind of money. There was no way I'd get there . . . I started crossing things off my 'wish list' until I got down to 300,000 *reais*.

The idea of saving so much is overwhelming at first, because it's a lot of money. Especially if you consider how I make it. Then it occurred to me to divide these 300,000 *reais* into instalments, to break it down so I wouldn't feel it so much. It was a simple calculation: 300,000 divided by 500 instalments = 600 *reais* per instalment. I got a piece of paper and numbered it from one to 500. This way, for every 600 *reais* I manage to save and deposit in my bank account, I cross off the corresponding number from the list. When there's nothing left to cross off, I'll know I've saved 300,000. Actually, I've already cut other things from my list and lowered the amount to 200,000. But I think I'll stop when I get to 100,000, even if it's not enough to buy a flat. At any rate, I've got my plans for the future. There are months when I managed to save as much as 8,000 *reais*. It looks like the future's on its way.

I'm going to have a few souvenirs from this period: two piercings (one in the navel, and one in my lower lip. I got rid of a third one, in my eyebrow) and three tattoos (my star-sign, the scorpion, on the back of my shoulder, a heart on my groin and a phrase on the back of my neck, which I had done for my ex-boyfriend – which I really regret: 'Thanks Du.' When we broke up, I had it changed to 'Thanks Dad').

As well as the things I'll be taking with me, there

are things I didn't achieve. I haven't studied in two years, and the feeling of having forgotten everything is inevitable. In fact, I'm sure I have. Before, I didn't like studying. I've changed my mind. I want to go to university as soon as all this is over. I'll finish my crammer course in 2005 and, if I get through the university-entrance exams, I want to enrol in psychology in 2006. I know lots of people who haven't been to university but they're in business and make a lot of money. They had help from their parents, though. Since I don't have this any more, I've realised that in order to get anywhere in life I'm going to have to study, whether I want to or not, whether I like it or not.

Tuesday, 28 December

FOURTH CLIENT

Today was my third time with these clients. Today they didn't want to go to a motel and came to my place. We had a good play. First, she did a quick strip, but it was enough to get the three of us turned on. Then I went down on her until she came in my mouth. But the part I liked the most was when she was riding him while I rimmed her. Ah yes – also when she went down on me while I sucked him off

. . . I had sex with him for a short while, but to my surprise, they went for it by themselves for quite a while, with me as a voyeur. I didn't come, although I really liked it when she went down on me. He didn't come either, because he was 'holding out'. But she came a lot! About four times, by my count.

It's funny. These days all of my friends are ex-clients. You never know you're going to be friends the first time. Like I've said before, I don't have sex with friends. Not personally, nor professionally. And I make this really clear.

Some are borderline – they're still my clients, but they border on becoming a friend. It's nice to receive their shows of affection. Lots of them call just to see how I am or, when I write in my blog, just to see if everything is OK. I also get a lot of presents. One guy gave me a CD that he'd personalised with a picture of me on the cover. It was fantastic! The other day, I wrote in my blog that I wanted to read *Angels and Demons* and a client bought me the book. Easter's also good, so is my birthday . . .

Last year, I celebrated my birthday in a swingers' club. At the time, I was really addicted to this type of place – being able to have sex with men and women, have loads of orgasms, the smutty atmosphere. A personal fixation, I confess. I thought: It's my birthday, I like the place, and there are stacks of people who've never had the courage to go to a swingers' club because they think it's just a brothel. So all those people who'd never had the courage had to go to a swingers' club that day. I had a boyfriend at the time and he went too – obviously! I wanted to bring everything together: birthday, fun, fantasies (mine with my boyfriend) and hang out with my friends. Fantasies indulged (mine and those of a lot of people, by the way). What a present!

Here in São Paulo there are lots of them. There are seven here in Moema alone! Outside, however, they look normal. They don't have 'swingers' club' written over the door. Like most people, I used to imagine that as soon as you walked in the door you'd see a lot of people in an orgy, naked, having sex. The night actually starts out as it would at a normal club: there are bars, tables, dance floors. That's where couples start to flirt, but nothing actually happens. It's only when you head towards the back of the house that things heat up. To get to the rooms, you have to go through a maze (not all clubs have this): a dark, really narrow corridor that makes everyone have to touch and rub against each other. You can have a lot of fun there, without feeling embarrassed, because you can hardly see who's there. A little further along are the rooms.

The walls are made of trestlework, so people outside can see everything that goes on inside (or whatever they're able to see, because the light isn't exactly like that of a football stadium). Everything is geared to being more tactile than visual. If you touch something and like it, go for it. It's really crazy – sometimes there are as many as twenty couples having sex at the same time. For shyer couples, who chatted each other up at the bar or on the dance floor, there are generally private rooms. They're for those who only want to swap with one other couple.

The down side of these places is that it's hard to find anyone really attractive. They are generally married couples, from thirty to forty-five years of age. Not really young, nor really old. There are several clubs that don't let prostitutes in. I've been barred from one. They assume the girls are only there for the money – and not the sex itself. They don't like that. The couples are looking to swap with other couples who are really married.

Thursday, 6th January

THIRD CLIENT

It was a normal session, nothing out of the ordinary. Afterwards, he told me he was turned on by sadomasochism. He's sadistic, let there be no mistake. Except he doesn't tell the girls over the phone because he likes to hit them when they don't expect it. He told me that when he got here he didn't have the courage to hit me. 'You don't look like a pro. You look too sweet and I didn't have the courage to hit you. I'm going to book another one tomorrow just so I can rough her up.' Just as well . . .

I've heard lots of stories of girls who find themselves in tricky situations while working. Out of sheer luck, I don't have many stories to tell. One of the things I feel most uncomfortable about in my work is charging my clients. I'm embarrassed. I've had two clients leave without paying – and without me charging them. In the ritual of a session, the money comes last. Like when you see the psychologist. In both these cases, I had to ask Gabi (who answers my mobile and makes appointments for me, because our voices are very similar) to call and charge them. Silly of me, isn't it? One of these 'unintentional runners' came back to pay. The other, who was already fairly far away, took my bank details and made a deposit. Decent folks. There were another two times at swingers' clubs: a Catalan of few words (not just because of the language, but because he really was the silent sort) took advantage of the fact that I'd gone to the bathroom and took off! The other one I forgive: I'd had a lot to drink and was sick, and I don't blame him for not wanting to pay.

It's funny, because it seems that there was a reason for this thing with money. After everything I'd done at home, to my parents, because of money, getting cheated a few times was a way of 'atoning' for it all. But other things also 'settled the score' for my bad behaviour. When I was still at the house on Alameda Franca, I had a friend, Taísa. She was pretty lazy and didn't make much money. Because I didn't have a bank account, I kept my money in a drawer. I noticed that money was always disappearing from there, but I never imagined it was her.

Even after we were kicked out of that house and had to work in the one in Moema, and the petty theft continued, I never had the courage to confront her. I didn't want to lose the friendship over money. One night, we went to a club in Vila Madalena. At the time, I was still doing coke. I also drank a lot that night, and got sick, obviously. In the bathroom, I thought she was helping me, but I felt her hand rummaging through my pocket. At the time, off my face, I didn't even click. When we went to pay I noticed my 50 *reais* were missing. I dragged Taísa into the bathroom, together with another girl, and gave her a complete search. Nothing. Then, using force, I made her take off her clothes and, surprise surprise . . . my 50 *reais* were rolled up in her knickers. It was the last straw. When we got to the brothel, I went upstairs to our room behind her, thinking she was going to kill me. Almost. There was lots of hair-pulling, scratching, slapping. I ended it, saying, 'You're just jealous because I work and you don't. But don't worry, tomorrow I'll make more.'

Another time I lost money was in my first flat. My savings of 3,000 *reais* simply disappeared. Gabi says that if it had happened to her, she would have been furious. I didn't even want to know if it was the maid or a client. Do you want to know the truth? I wasn't at all upset. I think, in a way, I'd finished paying for what I'd done. What goes around comes around . . .

Tuesday, 4 February

SECOND CLIENT

There have only been a few occasions where I've been so stunned I didn't know what to do. After all, I'm a professional. But this one was so weird that I decided not to do or say a thing. He came into my flat and didn't want to talk. He immediately started stripping, then took off my clothes and put on a condom. I think he'd walked in the door with a hard-on. He jumped on me in the missionary position and started frantically pumping away. There was just one thing: his dick wasn't inside me – he was just rubbing it against my groin. I lay there wondering the whole time if he just hadn't noticed or if it was his way of getting off. I thought it best not to ask. He might be offended. Or what if he thought that he was inside me and I was really loose? Who knows? Would you believe he actually came like that? And the strangest thing was that he kept asking, 'Are you enjoying yourself?' 'Mmm, delicious,' I answered. Then he asked, 'Did you come?' I wondered if he was joking . . . But I went along with him and said yes. It's difficult enough for a woman to come with a dick inside her, let alone outside!

I really think it's good when clients get things off their chest with me. There are girls who hate listening to clients' stories. But I think it's an important part of the 'package' for these men. They don't just come here to unload sperm. And they often tell you things they wouldn't confess to their friends or wives. There are some who, when the fright has worn off, are actually quite funny. One guy told me he'd just bought two bricks of mar-

ijuana. I gave him a scared look (and I really was).
He apologised, but said he just had to tell someone.
Another time, the client really wanted me to know
he was the 'big shit', a real gangster. The sex went
smoothly, however, with no frights. But when I
came out of the bathroom, I heard him talking on
his mobile. 'No. Make sure he's dead. Because if he
isn't, we're going to have to put an end to this.' He
used so much slang that I could barely understand
him. Staring straight at him, I thought he really did
look like a gangster. You know the ones you see on
TV, in the news? I started to cry, but without him
noticing. I was really frightened.

Other times, the fright is something else . . . I like
trying to guess what a guy's dick is like when he
arrives. Sometimes I get it right. Especially the
ones with small dicks. It's funny, but it seems to
be written on their faces. I don't know how to
explain it, although I'm right about 90 per cent of
the time. But the really well-hung ones are always
hard to pick. Some guys turn up and your imagination goes wild. But when the moment of revelation comes, not that it's small, but it's not the
monument you thought it was. And there are
others who, well, you'd never imagine. But when
it's unleashed, surprise surprise! There've been
moments when I've thought: It's not going to

out what it was like. It wasn't good because I saw that it really wasn't anything like what we imagine . . .

It also wasn't a good experience for other reasons. The pay is very bad. You don't make much at all. It's actually embarrassing to say how much I made, because it really is a pittance. OK: 500 *reais*. That's because this is Brazil. In the United States it's a profession. They treat you differently.

Everything that has happened in my life – the fame (fleeting, I know), the good and bad things, still frighten me in a way. The other day, I was walking down my street here, in dark sunglasses, when a passer-by came up to me (I actually thought he was going to mug me) and said, 'Excuse me. Forgive me for asking, but are you Bruna, the Surfer Girl?'

'No, I'm not.'

'Ah, sorry then, I was mistaken.'

I was really surprised. I'd never imagined someone would come up to me in the street, recognise me. I was so taken aback that I ended up saying I wasn't me. How silly . . .

On the other hand, I once went with a guy during a swap at a swingers' club, and he turned round afterwards and said, 'You're Bruna, the Surfer Girl, aren't you? I've always wanted to be your client, but now I've had you for free.' I wanted to kill the guy. Seriously.

What most surprises me is that usually people's reactions when they recognise me are neutral, although a few times I've heard sniggering when I go past. But I never know for sure if it was me they were laughing at, me they were talking about. I think it was, but I don't know why. But I'm not going to get neurotic because of the life I live. Or think a guy is flirting with me because he knows who I am. I'm a beautiful woman. I'm not going to think: Ah, he recognised me and that's why he's coming on to me. It's too crazy. I prefer to 'go with the flow'.

Sometimes, after midnight, I go to the building where my parents live. I stand on the pavement for ages. The last time, I went with my boyfriend. We spent half an hour there, drinking, while I watched the film in my head.

I see a girl in a school uniform coming out of the gate, carrying a bag with a few clothes in it. She looks frightened, disorientated, directionless – walking towards the fate she has chosen. I look up and see the windows with the lights out in the flat I once lived in. I remember the pastel-coloured walls of my room, the blinds (no curtains or cuddly toys – I have asthma and hay fever . . .), the

Babylândia furniture (I didn't want 'adult' furniture) and the large desk where I used to study and do my homework, and spend hours at my computer or watching TV.

I don't go there hoping to bump into them. I go when I do precisely so I won't see anyone. I'm not ready. Neither are they. How would my father react? And my mother? We've never spoken since. We'll meet again one day, I'm sure, but it will have to be planned. When I give up prostitution, I want to prove to them that I did it, but I stopped. I hope this will make it easier for them to accept me back into their lives.

When I finish my beer, I walk past the front of the building one more time, look around and see that a lot of things have changed. Including me.

I now see that everything I've been through was a phase I had to go through. No regrets. These three years had to be like this: prostitution, drugs . . . If it weren't like this, far from my parents, I might still be taking antidepressants. As for them, I have no idea . . . Why has it been good? The reasons are many (I always see the good side of things). I've matured as a person, learnt to look after and like myself, and I've learned to get along with all kinds of people, to respect them. I didn't used to respect anyone. If I hadn't been a prostitute, I'd never have learnt to accept people's differences. I've met all kinds of people, good and bad. The best one was Gabi. For all these reasons, I know I've become less selfish. I actually believe that if I'd been more patient, after a time, if I hadn't left home, my relationship with my parents would have gone back to normal one day. No Bruna, just Raquel. But only Bruna could have reached this conclusion. Raquel never . . .

Last year, I went to visit my grandmother, my mother's mother, who is in a geriatric hospital in Sorocaba. She showed me a photo album. There were no photos of my father in it. But there was one of my mother holding my newborn niece, who, for obvious reasons, I still haven't met. I don't know why, but I decided to borrow the photo and photocopy it. I keep it in my diary. In a way, it brings me closer to my mother – and maternity. I think about my own children (I want two – a boy and a girl, preferably twins). I imagine myself as a liberal mother who's friends with her kids. I'm living proof that locking them up and forbidding them to do things doesn't work. I'm going to let my kids come and go whatever time they want to, as long as I take them and pick them up. My own experiences have shown me where all the world's traps are. I fell into all of them.

Thursday, 21 May

. . . Sometimes I stop to think about what I've done in my life. I know I'll reap what I've sown, or perhaps it's already happening without me knowing. Today I went over my whole past, but I didn't get depressed, I just remembered things with nostalgia and affection. If it weren't for my past, I don't think I would have become the person I am. Not the pro, but the other side of me that few people know. It's so good to remember laughing with my family, holidays, friends from school, everything . . . After ages watching the 'film' of my past in my thoughts, I dried my tears and lifted up my head. I like to cry – it does me good.

BRUNA THE SURFER GIRL'S FORBIDDEN STORIES

I n almost three years in this business, by my count, I think I've had sex with more than 1,000 men. In theory it might not sound like a lot. But in practice . . . And I'm not just talking about the sex itself, but also having to deal with all kinds of men: handsome, ugly, nice-smelling, others less so, calm, hurried, macho, rude, sensitive. I can now say that no fantasy scares me any more, because I've seen and done everything. Some were a little weird, I admit. But I think the most important thing is that people shouldn't be ashamed or afraid to indulge their fantasies – no matter how unusual.

One day I went upstairs with an absolutely normal-looking client. In the bedroom, I'm not sure if I was able to hide my surprise when he said, 'Stick your fist in me.' He wasn't at all embarrassed about asking me to do it. He'd even come prepared. Jesus! I didn't think it would fit. I have a doctor friend who tells stories about the strange things that happen in the emergency ward, like when guys turn up with all manner of things up their rears ends that they can't get out. Bottles, which create a vacuum and refuse to come out, are the most common.

Well, I worked out that it wasn't impossible. If a long-neck beer bottle could make it in, a hand wasn't that much bigger. I realised the guy was very experienced at this. He took a surgical glove out of his briefcase and asked me to put it on. While he opened the package he said, without batting an eyelid, 'I bet you've never done this before.' Before I could say anything (that the expression on my face wasn't already saying) he went on, 'And I doubt you'll ever do it again. I want you to stick your fist in me.'

'OK, but you'll have to teach me how.'

'Put your fingers in one at a time until they're all in and keep pushing.'

I used a heap of KY . . . It won't go in all at once. I followed his instructions, and everything went in, quite easily, actually.

When my hand was inside him, up to the middle of my wrist, I remembered my doctor friend and was scared the client's anus might swell up until I couldn't get my hand out. Imagine me arriving at the hospital with my hand up the guy's arse! I confess, I was afraid we might make a mess or something. Not my cup of tea. 'Don't worry, I had a colonic lavage before coming here. There won't be any "accidents".' It didn't seem to be hurting him. By the way he was talking, the ease with which I stuck my whole hand in, and his obvious pleasure, I could tell this wasn't his first time.

I spent ages inside him, following his orders. 'A little more to the right, move it around.' I think I was there for more than half an hour, with my whole hand inside him, while he was on all fours on the ground, wanking himself off until he came – which took a long time. We didn't have sex.

In my work, I respect (and indulge) everyone's desires and fantasies, even if I don't accept some of them personally. So if a boyfriend of mine says he has this or that fantasy, I'm going to think he's lost the plot. And it's not going to happen! In my bed, outside of work, sex is liberal, but not that much!

~

I love a bit of a party. Not at swingers' clubs, but here at my place or a client's place. I've already participated in lots . . . One was unforgettable. Guess how many there were. Four? No. Five? No . . . EIGHT. And I was the only girl. It wasn't supposed to be just me. The guys, who were very young, had invited three other girls. It was going to be two dicks each. I was going to be the 'main course', since all of them wanted to spend some time with me. But when the other three arrived, they didn't like any of them and made me a proposal. 'What if we just have you? You up for it?' I agreed there and then.

I had to use a lot of creativity to handle them all, but luckily I've got a lot of that. It was going to be a first-class gangbang. They decided to go four at a time because lots of guys together would be too gay. It was the first four's turn. Those who know how to count will work out that I managed OK. First, musical cocks: with the four standing around me, I blew one on one side and another on the other, while I gave the other two hand jobs. Each one got a blow and hand job, in this order. But in gangbangs there's no such thing as organisation, queues, turn-taking.

Since the four of them were raring to go, the first one lay on his back and I rode him without letting go of the other three: one in each hand and the other in my mouth. Then the real merry-go-round began. We tried a variety of DPs, then as each one came he'd leave the room and call in the next one, who'd enter the fray, always starting with a blow and a hand job. Lucky for those who took a long time to come – or recovered quickly enough to go for another round. I came several times without much 'inner effort'. I took them down one at a time, all those stiff dicks. I don't even know how many rounds we did in the end. But the best part of all was that this was my most lucrative shag ever – eight at a time, and the money all to myself.

~

Some time ago, a client got pretty rough with me and I was a little shaken. What consoled me was knowing that the guy, who was already getting on in years, had never been married. I concluded that I wasn't the first – nor would I be the last – woman he'd treated badly. After he'd gone, I recorded his number on my mobile so I could avoid him in future. Time passed and every now and then he'd call me, but I didn't pick up.

Then one day he called me from a different number and gave me another name. As I didn't recognise his voice, I scheduled him in. I got a fright when I opened the door, and didn't know what to do. He came in, grabbed me and shoved me on to the sofa. At the time, I thought about everything except the money I'd be making. We went up to the bedroom, where he pushed me roughly on to the bed and started taking my clothes off . . . His sweaty hands on my body made me sick. He didn't even look like a man, but an animal. If I weren't a working girl, I'd have felt like a rape victim. But since I was, I just felt like shit.

I told him that if he kept being rough I'd have to stop. But he didn't even hear me. Either that or he pretended not to. I knew he'd be even more of a pain if I told him to leave, so I decided to keep going. I got on all fours and he rammed himself into me. It hurt a lot because I was drier than the Sahara desert and he was really hammering me as if I was an inflatable doll. Then he took his dick out of my pussy and stuck it in my arsehole. This hurt even more because it was also dry. I managed to reach the KY Jelly on the bedside table and wiped some on myself. He didn't like the fact that I was using KY, as if he was actually capable of getting a woman wet.

I stayed on all fours and he just didn't come. Each second felt like an eternity . . . I tried to keep it together, but I wasn't able to and started to cry. I'm not sure if I was crying with rage, hatred, pain or disgust. I think it was everything . . . Then I decided to stop, because I knew it wouldn't make any difference and might even make the situation worse. I tried to be strong and keep my anger under control.

I didn't make the slightest effort to pretend I was enjoying it. Why waste my breath on fake moans? I wanted him to know the truth – that I hated being there with him. Then he turned me over for the missionary position. My body was so limp I really did feel like a plastic doll . . . He stayed there on top of me for ages. At this stage in the game, knowing his time was almost up, all I could think about was the money. 'It's almost over,' I repeated mentally.

I don't know what went through his head. All I know is that my eyes were closed and he was still on top of me, when I felt him slap me across the face. I got a fright. I was even more frightened because I'd been caught by surprise. When he hit me the second time, I asked him to stop . . . Just as well he stopped after that, because I don't know what I might have done . . .

He kept going, and I couldn't stand it any longer – I was about to explode and do God knows what. I don't know, I'd have done whatever occurred to me at that moment. I didn't close my eyes again, so he couldn't catch me off guard. But I kept my face turned away . . . and it passed through my mind that, my father was the only man I'd let slap me across the face. But at that moment I saw that any man was capable of hitting me in the face . . .

Finally the hour was up. I got up and said it wasn't my fault he hadn't come. But what I could do was give him a hand job. And that's what we did. He got dressed, paid and left. I sat on the sofa and stared at the money for ages. All the anger I'd been feeling passed and was replaced with pity. Yes, because we should pity men like that, not be angry with them. He was a man who'd never been loved – he himself told me, the first time, that he'd never even been engaged. I know why. He doesn't need to say a thing because you can see in his eyes how sad and alone he is. And his aggressiveness in bed is just a reflection of the fact that he's never been loved.

~

A client came from out of town just to visit me. OK, so the town is close to São Paulo . . . But even though it's not very far, it was a big gesture, because there are pros in his town. But he came here for me. He belonged to some Oriental religion – I didn't catch the name properly. He even blessed me. We sat in front of one another holding our hands out and he said some things that I couldn't understand either . . . He told me he'd said a prayer for me to purify my spirit. And would you believe, it worked? It's true . . . I felt really relaxed afterwards. It's true.

Out of the blue, he asked, 'Would you like to meet Zequinha?' It took a minute for the penny to drop, but I said yes anyway. When he took off his pants, I understood that he called his dick Zequinha . . . Each to his own, right?

~

The best thing that happened at the swingers' club was meeting up again with a couple I'd met there three months before. The woman and I hadn't done anything; we'd just swapped partners. He's a really sexy guy in his forties – the sort I'm attracted to and would like for myself. A few grey hairs, a naughty look in his eye, great body – and good in bed. When I saw him, he was sitting down and I was on the dance floor. He smiled at me. Later, when she wasn't near by, he pulled me close and gave my neck and earlobe a lick and a few little nibbles, the sort that can't not turn you on. Discreetly, he handed me a card with his phone number on it and asked me to call him so we could meet up alone. But my client got jealous and didn't let me go with him.

I started something with a blonde, who was actually not bad . . . I was dying for some cunt, so I asked straight out if I could go down on her and she said yes. She sat down and I went down on her for quite a while, but she didn't come. While I was doing it, her husband kept caressing me – and I started to feel sick. I don't like it when men keep touching me while I'm with a woman.

But, on my other side, there was another woman who was touching me even more. It was a gentle touch, even though it was through my clothes. I could feel her softness.

She whispered in my ear, 'You're really sexy. Can I kiss you?'

My God! Why did she do that? I didn't think twice. I abandoned the blonde and leapt into the arms of the brunette, who was much sexier. We kissed a lot, I sucked her nipples a lot (she had silicone implants too), and she sucked mine. She talked dirty with me and I could tell she was turned on and acting naturally.

'I love young girls like you,' she said.

She must have been about thirty. I think we were together for more than half an hour . . . First, she went down on me until I came. Then I did the same to her.

We were really affectionate with each other, so much so that I made a point of saying goodbye to her. When I hugged her, I said, 'I really enjoyed being with you.'

Ah, how I'd like to meet her again somewhere else, without any men around. Just the two of us. I should have asked for her phone number. I don't know why but that woman fascinated me. So much so that I lost the desire for others.

~

My boyfriend and I were on our way home one night and we passed through an area where several transvestites turn tricks. I was a bit tipsy, and wanted to find out what kind of person picks up trannies. Nothing against transvestites. I think people can do whatever they want with their own body and it's no one else's business. I hung around a quiet street corner for about forty minutes. Pedro parked the car near by and kept out of sight so no one would realise he was keeping an eye on me.

It was pure adrenalin, because I was switched on to everything. I stayed on the lookout for transvestites who might want to ask me what I was doing there (after all, I might have been on someone else's corner), kept an eye on Pedro's car because it stands out, and checked out the people inside the cars that stopped . . .

I was really cold, because, even though I was wearing jeans, I only had a singlet T-shirt on . . . which brings me to the first thing I want to mention, because I've noticed that all transvestites work semi-naked, even when it's cold.

During the time I was there, more than ten cars stopped. I don't know exactly how many because I lost count after ten. Of the ones that stopped, only three really thought I was a transvestite; the others realised I was a woman.

It was funny because one stopped and said, 'You're a woman, aren't you?' I said yes, and he replied, 'Thank God . . . at last I've found one round here, but you're working the wrong corner, you know . . .'

There's one that I can't leave out. He thought I was a transvestite and even asked me how well-hung I was. We chatted a bit and I quickly noticed a ring on his left hand. I couldn't let this fact slip and asked if he was married. He said he was. So I asked if his wife knew he was in the habit of picking up transvestites and he answered, 'She has no idea I do this, nor must she ever find out!'

So someone likes transvestites. Fine . . . it's no-body else's business . . . but why marry a wo-man??? If they like transvestites, fine, but for Christ's sake, marry one. It's simple . . . I've heard so many stories of men who've married transves-tites and don't feel ashamed or guilty about it. Now these guys are real men! Because they own up to what they like . . .

Another car stopped with two young guys in it . . . They didn't let me down and realised I was a woman. I asked if they liked transvestites and they said in unison, 'No way, we like women.' There was one who stopped and asked right off if I was a transvestite. I said yes. He stared at my crotch and said, 'C'mon, it doesn't look like you've got a dick in there.' So I said, 'That's because it's limp.' But I couldn't contain myself and started to laugh, and he realised I was playing with him. There was also one who looked like a nutcase who said, 'How much for a quick blow job?'

To put the guys off picking me up, I hitched the price up. When the car wasn't all that hot, I told them my price was 100 *reais*, because I knew it would be too expensive. And when the car was better, I said it was 300, because even guys who looked like they had money knew this was a lot to charge in that area.

No one complained about my price, they just said they didn't have that kind of money on them, while some tried to haggle. One said, 'You're really worth it, but I've only got 40 *reais* in my wallet. Can't you do something for 40?' I laughed . . . and said no . . . because really, I wouldn't charge that even for a quick wank.

I really was charging a lot for someone who solicits on street corners, seeing as the people who do this charge 50 *reais* at the most. One guy said that no one he'd picked up on the street had ever charged him more than 40.

I had a bit of a laugh at an older guy's expense, but he didn't even notice. He stopped, thinking I was a transvestite, but when he got close, he looked me up and down and realised I wasn't. Even so, we chatted a while and I asked if he picked up trans-vestites very often. He said he did. I asked why he liked them and he replied that being with a trans-vestite satisfied his desire to be with a man and a woman at the same time. I asked if his arsehole was nice and stretched and he answered, very seriously (thinking I was being serious too), that he thought so, because it didn't hurt any more when he was getting buggered.

—

I once had a real smut session with two guys. One of them had already been my client. While I gave one a blow job, the other just watched us and wanked himself off. The one I was sucking off came in my mouth. Then I got to work on the other one and made him come like that too. I lay down and the two of them sucked on my nipples at the same time. Very nice. Meanwhile, I felt one of them masturbating me. I only didn't come because he doesn't know how to masturbate a woman. But I appreciated his intention . . .

I got on all fours, and while one gave it to me, I blew the other. At the same time. The one I was blowing came first, but the other one took a little longer. Being with two men really turned me on . . .

~

One night, at a swingers' club, I got with a sexy brunette. She was having sex with her partner and I sat next to her to touch her. I couldn't resist and started sucking her nipples, which were delicious. We kissed a lot, but it didn't go any further than that. I was dying to go down on her, but I didn't manage to pluck up the courage. We swapped partners and it was great. I enjoyed her partner and he gave it to me the way I like it. Unfortunately, he came quickly.

As we were leaving, I saw a really sexy blonde at a table, accompanied by an old man who could have been her grandfather, I swear. She grabbed me, but I noticed she was drunk. I stood in front of her and she slipped one of my breasts out and started sucking it. While she licked my nipple, she stared at me without blinking. Really nice stuff. But my client wanted to leave.

—

I answer the phone and the guy asks me straight up, 'Do you give brown showers?' Well, I'd given golden showers on several occasions, but I'd never given anyone a brown shower. I'll explain both. Golden showers are when the client asks you to pee on them, while he wanks off. Generally they prefer to have their shower after they've had a bit of sex so they can reach climax with their 'special request'. Of course, it's not easy. First, you have to drink a lot of beer and stay focused. You can't have sex with a bursting bladder – no woman is capable of that . . . You have to drink just the right amount so you can turn on the waterworks at your 'master's' command.

It's easier with shit. I did it once, and it was my first and last time. When the client asked me over the phone, I said I did it. More out of curiosity than desire. After all, how can we say we don't like something if we haven't tried it? So I did. I admit the situation made me a little nervous. The guy wanted to wank himself off while I did a 'number two' on him. He arrived, and there was a little foreplay, with him fingering my arsehole and playing with my bum. He didn't even want to fuck. We played around like this until I said I needed to go. Then he lay on his back, wanking frenetically, his eyes glued to my rear end, while I squatted over him, facing away. And I did it . . . Isn't that what he'd asked for?

—

I was about to jump on my client when we lay down, but he wanted to chat a bit beforehand because he liked the game of seduction, even with pros. Fine. We talked until he asked me if I kissed. I told him I didn't kiss all clients, just the ones I wanted to. Then I kissed him. He placed me face down on the bed and started licking and nibbling my back and bum. Then he turned me over and went down on me. Right after I'd come in his mouth, he kissed me and I could taste my juices . . . then he went down again, sucking my nipples, and kept going . . . tummy, pussy, legs and feet. On the way back up he went down on me until I came again. And gave me another kiss.

We put a condom on his dick, which was hard and throbbing, although I hadn't even touched him . . . He got me in the missionary position, but he started to go limp with the condom on. He told me he was used to having sex with his wife without a condom and when he had to put one on, he lost his hard-on. Normal. I wasn't fazed.

He asked me to do a sixty-nine with him so he'd get hard again. We did it for a while, but he couldn't get his hard-on back with his dick in a 'straightjacket'.

He wanted some time out to 'rest', so he went down on me again and I came for the third time. He came back to life and we put another condom on him, but he lost it again in no time . . . There was nothing we could do and our session ended for two reasons: one, because his time was up and two, because we couldn't have sex . . . Summing up: we didn't have sex, I came three times and made money doing it . . . aye aye . . . Even so, he said he'd be back.

—

One day I had a guy from London. He was really insecure and affectionate. There was a nice chemistry between us – and if I'd understood better what he was saying, we would have got along well, I'm sure. But the fun part was getting to see the Hotel Unique, where he was staying. Very chic! His room was really nice and had a plasma TV. We tried to talk a little in English, but then he started speaking Portunhol – a mix of Spanish and Portuguese. I had to keep asking him to repeat himself, because he spoke fast and I couldn't understand a thing. I thought he'd be aloof, like other foreigners. But he wasn't. On the contrary . . . He was even concerned that I had an orgasm. He went down on me for ages. I realised he wasn't going to stop until I got there. Pelvic-floor muscles, here we go! I asked him to lie on his stomach and started licking his back. The Englishman came to life and, surprise surprise, flopped over on to his back, offering me his arse, which I didn't refuse. I rimmed him until he was on fire. I took turns between his arse and his dick until he came.

~

Today I learnt two new positions: in the first one, the client made me lie on my back, with my legs up in the air as if I was about to roll backwards. Like a baby whose mother is going to dust his bottom with talcum powder. And while I did this he gave it to me in a squatting position. This was the one I liked best. I'd actually heard of the other, but I'd never tried it. It's called the scissor position. Both partners hold their legs apart, like two pairs of scissors joined at the groin. It's interesting, because you can use your partner's legs for support, pulling back on them. I recommend it.

~

Yes, I have had sex with famous people. It's funny how people think the famous don't have the urge . . . Relax – I'm not one to name names, nor will I ever be. Professional ethics. I'm a prostitute, not a blackmailer. When one guy arrived, I thought: I know this guy from somewhere. But the feeling went away. After all, we were there for something else. I didn't worry about trying to find out where I knew him from. But I realised he was a bit peeved that I hadn't said anything. Right in the middle of it, he trotted out, 'Your doorman asked me for an autograph.' Poor thing, he must have felt frustrated. I didn't say anything and kept sucking him off. I've never been impressed by fame, and wasn't about to start now. If he was expecting a shower of attention, a request for an autograph, or whatever, he didn't get it. And I don't believe in freebies for VIPs. After all, I was the star of that situation . . .

Another famous person was a TV presenter. It was easy-going, couple sex that later got smutty. I knew (and he knew I knew) who he was, of course. Introductions weren't necessary.

～

A real girlie party. Just me and three other women, without any men around. They've all got plump pussies the way I like them. While we all gently take each other's clothes off, an array of exciting lingerie appears, along with implants and natural breasts – all different, but just as sexy. Small nipples, pointy nipples, but no 'pancakes' – just succulent breasts, which you can feel, stroke, suck.

We form a daisy chain, each one nuzzling her mouth into the next one's pussy, until the circle is closed and no one is left out, giving and receiving affection and pleasure at the same time. We take turns. Each one has a different smell and flavour. At one stage, I become the centre of attention. There are three women serving me: one licks my breasts, another goes down on me and the third one positions herself over my face and offers me the best of herself, so I can lick her, suck her and make her come.

The sequence of orgasms is incredible. Moans become the musical backdrop for this women's party. There are no fake dicks, dildos. Just a feminine touch, delicate mouths, expert tongues, the rubbing of skin, breasts, cunts. And we have wave after wave of orgasms until we're exhausted, but satisfied. Then we rest in each other's arms until we've caught our breath and start all over again.

Well, this is my sexual fantasy. Unfortunately, it has never happened, except in my imagination. One day it's going to be a memory that'll make me wet just thinking about it.

There's another fantasy I hope to fulfil one day – to have sex with a military policeman. But he has to be from here in São Paulo. That uniform of theirs drives me crazy. The cut makes any man look sexy. Hasn't anyone noticed? It makes their bums look high and tight, and the bulge between their legs is concentrated in such a way that you can see they're sporting a lethal weapon. Their shirts and jerseys give them a very sensual shape, and they wear black boots with large buckles. Mmm.

The sex would be wild, with him dressed (of course!) and me running my hands over his entire body, as if I'd just been given a new doll to play with, so later he'd grab me forcefully, but not violently, and do whatever he wanted with me. Him doing me up against a wall with my legs wrapped around his waist. Just the thought of a military cop dropping his trousers to fuck me, wow . . . I'd confess things I'd never done. If all this happened in public, in a cinema, for example, it would be paradise. Having sex in public, or knowing someone's watching me, I'd be halfway towards a historical orgasm. Indulging two fantasies at once would be divine. Well, now I've confessed my most secret desires, maybe they'll come true? Any takers?

BRUNA THE SURFER GIRL'S TIPS ON HOW TO SPICE UP YOUR SEX LIFE

I always wonder why so many men come looking for prostitutes. I've noticed that couples don't talk much these days, especially about sex. They don't tell each other what they like (and what they don't like), their fantasies. But you can't force someone to do something they don't want to: it takes two to have sex. Some hard-core fantasies scare wives (or can even put an end to marriages). That's why they come to us . . . Yes, women are good wives and mothers, companions, confidantes and friends. But in bed they should try to loosen up and have a good fuck. It'll do them good, I promise.

I hope sharing my experience will make it a little easier for people. Here are just a few tips, simple things to spice up this game for two (or three, or four . . .).

UNPLANNED SEX

There's nothing weirder than scheduled sex . . . Of course I schedule in my clients. But with a real partner, the best part is the element of surprise. Try to catch them off guard, forgetting about time and place (as long as it's not in public): in the bathroom, kitchen, on the stairs of your building. Prohibited places where you feel you might get caught give you a rush of adrenalin that sensualises everything.

THE GAME OF SEDUCTION

To spice up a relationship, forget 'every Saturday night', OK? But there are other basic tricks, like the woman putting on some really sexy lingerie (sometimes just a suspender belt is enough to 'suspend' her partner's breath), a costume (nurse, plumber, flight attendant . . .). A two-way strip-tease (taking turns removing an item of clothing) can help people with their fear of looking ridiculous (and since when has seducing someone been ridiculous?).

TOYS

A visit to a sex shop will open the door to a world of possibilities, I promise. No, they don't just sell rubber dicks. Although that can be an interesting place to start. Fly higher: use handcuffs, blindfold each other, play with smells and sensations, your sense of touch. These shops carry all kinds of stimulating gels, which can really get things sizzling. A good reason to give each other a mutual massage – the sort that relaxes and lights your fire at the same time. A good porn film on DVD can heat things up. But don't forget – all this is to make foreplay pleasurable and get both of you in the mood for a hot fuck. But it won't work if it's only two minutes then 'down to business'.

INTENSITY

Some people think sex should be like in porn films: the guy wildly banging the girl as if he were drilling through asphalt. You might actually get to this point, but not straight off. The fun part is varying the intensity. One day, it might be gentle. The next day, wilder. Or both on the same day. But unvarying sex, always following the same script, becomes routine.

ORAL FOR MEN

Something that should never be left out for either partner. It's different and stimulating. It's what I most like in bed (whether giving – which, all modesty aside, I do very well – or receiving it). Some clients joke with me, saying I should give other women lessons on how to do it. Well, here's part of the secret: play a lot with your tongue around the head of the penis, and every now and then put a little pressure on it with your mouth. Don't just masturbate the guy with your hand. The exciting part of oral sex is precisely making the most of the possibilities: lips, tongue, teeth (very lightly), suction (which is exactly what the vagina does), the space in your mouth. Good oral sex is when the woman doesn't use her hands and does all the work with her mouth.

I always start by sucking their balls, which is a very sensitive, pleasurable area for men. I alternate between licking and sucking gently (remember, the balls are very sensitive, so don't try anything that might hurt), while I slowly make my way up to the penis. While I perform oral sex, I imagine my mouth is a vagina swallowing the penis. I do this on purpose. They cotton on and imagine they're ramming it into a vagina, but at the same time they know they're going to come in a woman's mouth. Oral sex has to be wet, with the tongue playing a lot around the penis, like a child eagerly sucking a lollipop. When he comes, don't be disgusted – keep sucking to the last drop.

The intensity of oral sex varies from man to man (and you need to find out what his rhythm is). Some like slow, careful movements. Others like it fast. How do you know how he likes it? Easy: try both ways and see which one makes him moan more intensely with pleasure, when he starts to writhe.

ORAL FOR WOMEN

Oral on women is a little more complicated (pay attention, guys). I'd say 80 per cent of my clients have performed oral sex on me. Of these, only 10 per cent know what they are doing. Of course, good oral sex for one woman is bad for another, since each woman feels pleasure in a different way and place. But knowing this is already a great step forward. Some feel pleasure in the clitoris, others in the labia, while yet others feel it in the vaginal canal. So, guys, the best thing is trial and error: explore each of these regions and pay attention to her reaction. You'll know when you're on the right track . . .

The intensity also varies from person to person. Some women prefer light licks. Others like it to be harder, with a few little nibbles (or not – she's the one who will say how hard she likes it). I prefer the tongue on my clitoris, with fast, strong licking movements. And no soft tongues! The tongue should be like my finger when I masturbate. In my blog, I always joke that there are three kinds of lickers. And, of course, I have my preferences. Want to know how I classify them? The first is what I call 'the dog with a slab of meat in his mouth'. These are the guys who stick their faces in your cunt and shake their heads back and forth. A lot of the time you can't even feel their tongue, just their nose. A word of advice for these guys: in my case, at least, it doesn't turn me on even remotely . . . I get tense and worry that I'm going to get bitten or hurt. The second type is what I call 'the ice-lolly'. They're like kids sucking an ice-lolly, licking up and down without stopping anywhere. It can be a turn-on, but you need a good deal of concentration and 'inner effort' to reach orgasm this way. The third is the sort that licks like a woman. Guys, don't lose heart: women really do know what other women want. It's hard to explain. They know how to find the right spot with their tongues, with the right intensity, and their fingers go precisely to that unexplored region known as the G-spot. So, guys, if you really want to give a woman good oral sex, don't be too shy to ask how. We'll tell you everything . . .

Now the best position, of course, is the sixty-nine: you can give and receive oral pleasure at the same time. It can be with her on top, with him on top (careful: in this position, some guys think they can pump away to their heart's content . . .), or both lying on their sides.

ANAL SEX

A lot of women email me asking how to go about having anal sex. They say they really want to but are (unanimously) afraid of feeling pain, or they say they've tried but haven't managed to go all the way. My advice: ask your partner to lie on his back and you get on top. This way you will be able to control the penetration, movement and rhythm – as much or as little as you can take. A lubricant gel can help with the penetration.

For men, my advice is different: be patient. Let the woman take the lead and choose the position she is used to (or let her discover what she likes if she's never done it before). For those who are already adept, the best position really is on all fours, because it's more pleasurable for the woman. Beginners should not try this. It's dangerous for a man to ram it in all at once, as I've had happen to me. It wasn't nice . . .

Another question about anal sex that crops up time and again is hygiene. It's not very nice to see a mess on the condom afterwards. This kind of accident can be avoided. The only way to eliminate the risk is by using a vaginal douche, which you can buy at a chemist. It is a rubber device in the shape of a pear, with a plastic tube that you fit to the top. All you do is fill the rubber base with water and slide the tube into the anus. You squeeze the rubber part until all the water is inside you. Then you let the water come out by itself, removing anything that's inside. It doesn't hurt and allows you to have clean anal sex.

But if, after all that, something still comes out, no matter how embarrassing it is (and it is, I promise), the guy has to understand that this hole was actually made for something else . . . With this lavage, there is almost no risk.

A tip for the boys: please don't try to go straight to the main course. Women need to be in the mood for anal sex. So concentrate first on her pleasure (so yours will be just as good). Lots of caressing, oral sex, get her to relax . . . Then you'll both come, a lot. If only one of you comes, the sex wasn't complete.

BRUNA'S FIFTEEN COMMANDMENTS

1) Be liberal in bed and don't be shy in the privacy of your bedroom.

2) Indulge all your fantasies with your partner, with respect and affection. And take turns: today your fantasy, tomorrow, your partner's.

3) Go to sex shops together to see what's new on the market. Even if you don't buy anything, it's worthwhile just for the fun of it.

4) Try different places. You can't only have sex in bed now, can you?

5) Vary the intensity and style of sex: lovers, wild, gentle, hurried . . .

6) Lots of foreplay, always: this is the most inter-active part of sex.

7) Never have a set day, time or script (kiss first, oral on her, oral on him and down to business . . .).

8) Investigate your partner's body, without limits: feet, the nape of their neck, stomach . . . find out what turns them on.

9) Never try to get someone to do something they don't want to – respect their limits. If you want to cross them, talk a lot, make your partner relax, lead them gently.

10) Always make sure the woman comes first so she gets turned on and ready for everything else.

11) If you can't work out how your partner prefers something, ask gently.

12) Show love and affection afterwards – talk, smoke a cigarette or just hold one another. Coming, rolling over and going to sleep is the pits . . .

13) Don't fake orgasms just to make your partner happy. If it didn't happen, it didn't happen.

14) Discover new positions. Missionary every day – no way.

15) If you have a fantasy that will definitely frighten your partner or make them think you're depraved, the best thing to do is find a professional who can satisfy you.

EPILOGUE

Bruna Surfistinha retired from working as a call girl just before her twenty-first birthday and is now studying to read psychology at university. She intends to continue her blog until the day she dies. She wants to write 'Tomorrow I am getting married' and 'My baby was born yesterday' and truly hopes that these things will happen with Pedro. 'I was lucky enough to meet the man of my dreams while I was working as a prostitute. Not everyone has such a happy ending.' Meanwhile, she believes that the most important thing in life is always to strive for happiness.

The Scorpion's Sweet Venom is being translated into twelve languages, published worldwide and made into a film.